*Floating Like A*

**JELLYFISH**

*Floating Like A*

*JELLYFISH*

*The Entrepreneur's Dance with Failures, Goals, and Successes*

Written By:  Sherry Kelly

**Copyright © 2025 by Sherry Kelly**

All rights reserved. No part of this book may be reproduced, distributed, or transmitted in any form or by any means, including photocopying, recording, or other electronic or mechanical methods, without the prior written permission of the publisher, except in the case of brief quotations embodied in critical reviews and certain other noncommercial uses permitted by copyright law. For permission requests, write to the publisher at the address below:

Published by: Sherry Kelly

ISBN: 979-8-218-60063-1

First Edition

Printed in the United States of America

## Disclaimer

Disclaimer

This book is based on my personal experiences and journey as an entrepreneur and licensed hair stylist in two states. The content shared here is intended for informational and motivational purposes only. While I am a licensed professional in the hair and beauty industry, I am not a doctor, lawyer, therapist, or financial advisor.

The insights, stories, and advice offered in this book are my own and may not apply to every reader's situation. Any life or business-altering decisions you choose to make based on the content of this book are entirely your responsibility. I am released from any liability for negative or adverse outcomes that may result from such decisions.

Before making significant choices regarding your health, finances, legal matters, or business, I encourage you to seek guidance from qualified professionals.

This book is meant to inspire and motivate you to pursue your own goals and dreams. Your journey is uniquely yours, and I wish you great success in your endeavors!

# Dedication

Dedication

To the dreamers who refuse to give up, to the entrepreneurs navigating uncertain paths, to my husband, daughter, and grandkids who sacrificed time with me so I could follow this path, your unwavering support and love have been my anchor through every challenge and triumph. This book exists because of your belief in me, even when the journey took me away from precious moments with you.

And to anyone who needs a reminder that they are capable of greatness... This book is for you, a testament to resilience, love, and the power of dreams. May it inspire you to pursue your path with courage and heart.

## Table of Contents

1. **The Spark of a Dream: How Passion and Purpose Ignited My Journey**
    - Finding inspiration in everyday moments
    - Recognizing the gap in the market for natural, effective products
2. **Foundations of Courage: Launching a Solo Salon**
    - Transitioning from employee to business owner
    - Building trust with clients while creating a unique salon experience
3. **The Hurdles of Launching a Business During a Pandemic**
    - Navigating shutdowns, regulations, and limited resources
    - Creative problem-solving to keep the dream alive
4. **The Setbacks That Built Me: Transforming Obstacles into Strength**
    - Facing financial and emotional struggles

- Learning to adapt and pivot when things don't go as planned
5. **Developing a Resilient Mindset: Thriving When Times Get Tough**
    - Embracing failure as part of the process
    - Using affirmations, reflection, and mindfulness to stay grounded
6. **The Power of Staying True to Your Vision: Building a Brand That Matters**
    - How authenticity became the cornerstone of my businesses
    - Balancing innovation with staying aligned to core values
7. **Self-Care: The Secret Weapon of Entrepreneurs**
    - Daily rituals to manage stress and increase productivity
    - Setting boundaries between work and personal life
8. **Lessons Learned from Being "Taken": Safeguarding Your Business**
    - Red flags to watch for in partnerships and deals
    - Turning painful lessons into actionable strategies for growth

9. **Reflecting on Success and Reframing Failure: A New Perspective on Growth**
    - How to define success beyond monetary outcomes
    - Finding the silver linings in every setback
10. **Staying Inspired and Motivated Through Challenges: The Entrepreneur's Toolkit**
    - Cultivating creativity and keeping the fire alive
    - Networking and surrounding yourself with supportive communities
11. **Goal Setting: Turning Dreams into Achievable Milestones**
    - Establishing long-term goals and the power of micro-actions
    - Tracking progress and celebrating wins—big and small
12. **Becoming (or Maintaining) Entrepreneurial Status: A Lifelong Commitment to Growth**
    - Staying ahead of trends and embracing ongoing education
    - Building a legacy that inspires others

13. **Advice to My Younger Self: Wisdom from the Journey**
    - Overcoming self-doubt and believing in your unique path
    - Key lessons that shaped my career and personal growth
14. **Turning Dreams Into Legacy: Leaving a Mark Beyond Business**
    - Transforming a passion project into a lasting legacy
    - Mentoring others, giving back, and creating a ripple effect of impact
    - Building something that endures and inspires the next generation

# PREFACE

Preface

Starting my solo salon, Studio Di Capelli, and launching Caruso Valore (Hair & Skin Care) during the height of the pandemic was nothing short of a rollercoaster. What began as a dream to create a space where people could feel truly seen and cared for quickly evolved into something much deeper than I could have ever anticipated. I never imagined that the quiet moments of reflection in my salon—those moments when I could connect with clients on a more personal level—would lead to the growth of my solo salon and the birth of Caruso Valore. Yet, it was in those very moments, amidst the chaos of a global crisis, that I realized just how essential it was to create a space and products that not only supported my health but could also make a meaningful impact on my clients' lives.

The journey to this point has been filled with both triumphs and setbacks, with every challenge offering an opportunity for growth. From navigating the uncertainty of the pandemic to adjusting to the ever-evolving landscape of entrepreneurship, I've learned more than I ever thought possible—not just about business, but about myself. The process has transformed me in ways I never expected, deepening my understanding of what it truly means to be an entrepreneur and the role that self-care plays in that process.

There were moments when I felt completely overwhelmed, staring at a mountain of uncertainty. The salon I had worked so hard to build was suddenly at risk of shutting down, only a few months after opening its doors, and launching a product line in the midst of a global crisis seemed like an impossible feat. But through every low, I found a new layer of resilience. I learned that resilience isn't just about bouncing back from failure; it's about leaning into the discomfort, trusting the process, and having the courage to continue moving forward even when the path ahead is unclear.

During the toughest times, I learned that entrepreneurship is not a solo journey. It's about building a support system—a network of people who believe in you, encourage you, and hold you accountable. For me, that network included my family, clients, mentors, and fellow entrepreneurs who shared their wisdom, offered their support, and reminded me to keep going. In the midst of the pandemic, I found strength in these connections and in the realization that we are all navigating uncertainty in our own ways.

But it wasn't just external support that got me through—it was the inner strength I developed through the challenges I faced. Self-care became a non-negotiable part of my routine. As a business owner, I quickly realized that I could not pour from an empty cup. Taking care of my body, mind, and spirit was essential, not just for my own well-being, but also for the success of my business. This book is as much about entrepreneurship as it is about the importance of self-care. Without a healthy balance, the dream of building something meaningful will always feel just out of reach.

Through the process of launching my solo salon and Caruso Valore, I discovered that my story is not just my own. It's a story that resonates with so many entrepreneurs and dreamers who, despite the challenges they face, refuse to give up. I hope that as you read these pages, you see parts of your own journey reflected in my story. Whether you're just starting out or already navigating the complexities of entrepreneurship, I want you to feel that you're not alone. Your dreams matter, and they are worth fighting for.

This book is my gift to you—a reminder that no dream is too big, and no obstacle is insurmountable. It's a testament to the power of resilience, the importance of self-care, and the unwavering belief that you can turn your passion into something extraordinary. I hope you find comfort in knowing that your journey—no matter how challenging—is valid, and that with the right mindset, you too can build something that aligns with your purpose.

As you move forward in your own entrepreneurial endeavors, remember that it's okay to stumble, to feel lost at times, and to question your path. But also remember that the moments of doubt and struggle are where you'll find your strength. Trust in the process, trust in your vision, and above all, trust in yourself. You are capable of more than you realize.

This book is not just a story about my journey; it's a shared experience. My hope is that, as you read, you'll find inspiration, motivation, and practical guidance to help you navigate your own entrepreneurial challenges. May it serve as a reminder that, no matter where you are on your path, you are on the right track.

# Introduction

Introduction:

It could be said that I was always in search of something more; the perfect job. Perhaps it was an inner need for growth and a desire to expand my knowledge base that led me down this path of having so many jobs over the years.

I saw each successive position as an opportunity to learn something new, whether it was developing my interpersonal skills or honing my technical knowledge. I was never afraid to take a chance on something different, and with each job change, I gained invaluable experience that made me more well-rounded.

In some ways, having so many jobs enabled me to better understand the working world and the unique problems associated with different industries. It gave me a deeper appreciation of the value of hard work and perseverance, since I was able to see first-hand how things worked in each job.

Although it may have seemed like a lot of change at first, I'm grateful for all the experiences that my job exploration has brought me. It enabled me to grow as an individual and develop skills that will continue to serve me well into the future. I now have a better understanding of what I want out of my career, and I'm confident that I can achieve it.

This experience also made me realize the importance of networking and staying connected with previous colleagues. Having strong relationships is key to success since you never know when an old contact may be able to help you out or vice versa. It also demonstrates that you are someone who is committed to their career and takes initiative.

Ultimately, my job exploration has been a great learning experience that I would highly recommend to others. It may seem daunting at first, but the rewards are invaluable and will pay off in the long run. With a bit of courage and perseverance, you can make great strides in your career and open up a whole new world of possibilities.

Think about it—why limit yourself to one job when there are so many opportunities waiting to be explored? Take the time to research different roles, connect with people in industries that spark your interest, and see where your curiosity leads you. Who knows—your next big breakthrough could be just around the corner!

Every job is an adventure, and each new experience can teach you something valuable. But let me be clear—**this is not to say you should quit your current job** or make impulsive decisions. This is about realizing you're not as stuck as you might feel. It's about planning a thoughtful path forward and finding what truly fits you best.

For years, I struggled with the idea that moving from one job to the next meant I was failing. I'd hear comments like, "You need to stick it out," or "Quitting again? That doesn't look good." It weighed on me, and I doubted myself so many times. But looking back now, I see how each role I took, each pivot I made, taught me something about myself. Those experiences weren't failures—they were stepping stones that helped me discover my passion and unlock my entrepreneurial spirit.

What others saw as instability, I turned into an exploration of what truly aligned with me. It took time—years, honestly—but I turned those doubts into clarity and built something meaningful.

This book will teach you how to reflect on your own experiences and learn from them—especially if you're already in the entrepreneurial mindset, which you must be if you're reading this. Whether you're exploring a new idea, starting a business, or simply seeking something that feels more aligned with your passions, looking back at your journey can reveal hidden lessons and strengths.

This is about inspiring the entrepreneur in you. It's about understanding that taking control of your career, even in small ways, can open doors you never knew were there. Start by exploring what excites you—whether it's learning a new skill, diving into a passion project, or researching an industry that sparks your curiosity. You don't have to quit your job to begin. Sometimes, it's about planting the seeds of something new while still building from where you are now.

Turning what feels like a negative—being unsure or restless—into something positive is possible. Every experience, even the tough ones, can teach you something that helps you grow. It's not about perfection; it's about persistence and curiosity.

**Market Competition:** Most industries are highly competitive, making it challenging to stand out and succeed.

However, despite these challenges, entrepreneurship can also be incredibly rewarding. It offers the opportunity to pursue your passion, create something meaningful, and have control over your destiny. It can lead to financial independence and personal growth.

If you're considering becoming an entrepreneur, it's essential to do thorough research, develop a solid business plan, seek mentorship, and be prepared for the ups and downs of the journey. It's not for the faint of heart, but for those with the right mindset and determination, it can be a fulfilling and successful path.

"Becoming an entrepreneur is not for sissies. It's a path filled with challenges, risks, and uncertainties that demand unwavering determination and resilience. While entrepreneurship offers the promise of personal fulfillment, financial independence, and the opportunity to bring your ideas to life, it also requires the courage to face setbacks, make tough decisions, and work tirelessly to achieve your goals. In this demanding journey, only those with the fortitude to navigate the turbulent waters of business can hope to find success."

work and personal life can be challenging.

**Decision-Making:** Entrepreneurs must make critical decisions regularly, often with incomplete information. These decisions can have a profound impact on the success or failure of the business.

**Financial Pressure:** Managing cash flow, securing funding, and ensuring the business stays financially viable are constant concerns for entrepreneurs.

**Adaptability:** The business environment is ever-changing. Entrepreneurs need to adapt to new technologies, market trends, and competition continuously.

**Persistence:** Facing setbacks and failures is a common part of entrepreneurship. It takes resilience and determination to keep going when things get tough.

**Wearing Many Hats:** In the early stages of a business, entrepreneurs often have to handle various roles, from marketing and sales to operations and customer support.

potential employers or mentors. With the right preparation and dedication, you can reach your goals in no time - so don't wait any longer - get started now!

A little insight:

Becoming an entrepreneur can indeed be a challenging and demanding path. It requires a unique combination of skills, traits, and qualities, and it's not suited for everyone. Here are some reasons why entrepreneurship can be tough:

> **Risk and Uncertainty:** Entrepreneurship often involves significant financial and personal risk. There's no guarantee of success, and you may face financial setbacks along the way.
> **Responsibility:** As an entrepreneur, you're responsible for every aspect of your business, from the big-picture strategy to the smallest details. This can be overwhelming.
> **Long Hours:** Many entrepreneurs work long hours, especially in the early stages of their businesses. Balancing

So, take a deep breath, look at where you are, and start dreaming of where you could go. The entrepreneur in you is waiting—let them out and see where the journey takes you.

The world is full of possibilities - all you have to do is explore and with the right attitude, dedication, and a bit of luck, you can make your dreams come true. So don't wait - get out there and start discovering what really resonates with you. Who knows what you'll find - it could be the beginning of something magical.

Finally, never forget that you are capable of achieving great things. With hard work and determination, you can make strides in your career and open up a whole new world of possibilities. So don't be afraid to explore the unknown, and push yourself out of your comfort zone - it could be the best decision you ever make!

Good luck on your entrepreneurial exploration journey - I wish you all the success! Maybe you want to or already are an entrepreneur...with that said, the best way to stay on track is to set a goal and create a plan to achieve it. Identify your skills, research different industries, and use networking tools to get connected with

Floating through life like a jellyfish can be both a serene and contemplative experience, but it also raises questions about one's sense of purpose and agency. The gentle, rhythmic drift of a jellyfish in the ocean currents might symbolize a state of peaceful surrender to the flow of life, where you let go of the need to control every aspect of your journey. It can be a time of reflection and self-discovery, a moment to recharge and find inner peace.

However, it's essential to strike a balance. While the jellyfish's tranquility is admirable, it's equally crucial to remain proactive and not simply wait for magic to happen. Life often requires a mix of passive acceptance and active pursuit of goals, dreams, and opportunities. So, floating like a jellyfish may offer temporary respite, but the magic truly happens when you engage with life, shaping your destiny as you go with the currents.

It can be a soothing experience, but it contrasts starkly with the challenging journey of becoming an entrepreneur. While the jellyfish embodies calmness and surrender, entrepreneurship demands ambition, determination, and hard work. Aspiring entrepreneurs often find themselves navigating turbulent waters, facing obstacles, uncertainties, and taking calculated risks. Unlike the passive drift of a jellyfish, entrepreneurs must actively chart their course, adapt to changing conditions, and make strategic decisions.

Success in entrepreneurship doesn't typically manifest magically; it emerges through dedication, innovation, and relentless effort. So, while the allure of floating peacefully like a jellyfish may be tempting, the path to becoming an entrepreneur is a dynamic, demanding voyage that requires more than passive acceptance—it demands active engagement with the challenges and opportunities that arise along the way.

# Chapter One

Chapter One

**Chapter 1: The Spark of a Dream**

Every business starts with an idea—sometimes a flash of inspiration, sometimes a slow-burning realization. For me, the spark that ignited the dream of launching my own hair and skin care line, Caruso Valore, wasn't a single moment, but a series of observations, conversations, and reflections that evolved over time. It all began in my salon, a space where I had the privilege of working closely with my clients every day. Each cut, each style, and each conversation provided valuable insights into their lives, their concerns, and, ultimately, their needs.

As I spent time with clients in the chair, I began to notice a recurring theme. Many of them, despite their love for beauty products, were increasingly frustrated with the lack of options available that didn't contain harsh chemicals or synthetic ingredients. They would share stories of sensitive skin, scalp irritation, and frustration over finding products that would enhance their beauty without compromising their health. Some were even using "natural" products, only to find out later that they weren't as pure as advertised. Their disappointment and desire for healthier, more effective options stuck with me.

One day, a client sat in my chair and started telling me about how her skin had become more sensitive since she had switched to a more eco-conscious lifestyle. She mentioned that she had spent hours scouring the shelves for a shampoo that would be gentle on her hair but still worked effectively. She had found some "organic" shampoos, but they left her hair dry and lifeless. Other products were filled with fragrance and chemicals that irritated her skin. As she spoke, I began to feel the weight of the gap in the market. There were plenty of options, but none seemed to offer the balance of natural ingredients, effectiveness, and real care that my clients needed.

At that moment, I realized that my role as a stylist was more than just providing a great cut or color—it was about offering solutions that aligned with my clients' overall well-being. The desire for a natural, effective product line wasn't just a passing thought—it was a need that I could help fill. And with that realization, the vision for Caruso Valore Hair and Skin Care was born.

I spent days thinking about how I could create a line that would address these concerns. What if I could develop products that were not only good for the skin and hair but also good for the soul? Products that were natural, but still effective—products that didn't rely on chemicals, fillers, or artificial ingredients. What if I could offer something that could help people feel better inside and out?

The more I reflected on this idea, the more I saw how it could bring a fresh perspective to the hair and skin care market. The industry was flooded with options, but most of them came with hidden ingredients that didn't align with the growing demand for transparency and health-conscious choices. This realization helped me sharpen my vision: Caruso Valore would offer high-quality, natural products that were both effective and good for the health of my clients.

But the idea of starting a product line was daunting. Where would I even begin? How would I source ingredients? How would I handle packaging, marketing, and distribution? The questions seemed endless, but the drive to create something meaningful kept pushing me forward.

As I began to explore the concept further, I realized that my salon experiences were not just the backdrop to this idea—they were the foundation. The deep connection I had built with my clients gave me valuable insights into what they truly wanted. And through these relationships, I could not only create a product that filled a gap in the market but also create something that had a personal touch, something that was born out of care and connection.

**Turning Passion into a Business Concept**

Many entrepreneurs feel the pull of a passion project, but translating that passion into a viable business concept can be overwhelming. It requires careful reflection, planning, and a willingness to take risks. For me, this wasn't just about making a product—it was about creating something that could improve people's lives in a meaningful way. This chapter is about helping you tap into your own "spark" and start the process of transforming your passion into a tangible business idea.

**Exercise: Identify Your Spark**

Before you can build your dream business, it's important to reflect on the moment or series of moments that sparked your entrepreneurial journey. What was it that inspired you to pursue this path? Was it a personal experience, a need you saw in the world, or a challenge you faced? Understanding the roots of your passion will help you turn it into a viable business concept.

*Take a moment to reflect on a pivotal moment in your life where a desire to create something meaningful was born. Write it down—what did you want to change or improve, and why?*

1. **What problem or challenge did you notice in your life or the lives of others?**
2. **How did this problem make you feel?**
3. **What action did you take to address this challenge, even in a small way?**
4. **What skills, knowledge, or experiences do you have that could help you address this need or problem in a meaningful way?**

This exercise isn't just about identifying the initial spark—it's about building a deeper understanding of the "why" behind your passion. By knowing why you want to create something and how it connects to your values, you can begin to shape your idea into something that feels authentic and aligned with your purpose.

**Building on the Vision**

Once you've identified your spark, the next step is to build on that vision. For me, the vision for Caruso Valore wasn't something I immediately saw as a fully formed product line. It was a feeling, a desire to create something meaningful that would resonate with others. It took time to nurture that vision and give it structure, and this process will look different for everyone. It might start with a simple sketch, a conversation, or a journal entry, but with time, patience, and hard work, that initial spark can grow into something bigger than you imagined.

Reflection Questions:

1. What early experiences or challenges shaped the vision for your business?
2. How did you feel when you first identified the need or gap in the market?

3. What does your ideal business look like, and what impact do you want it to have on the world?
4. How does your business concept align with your personal values and goals?

By reflecting on these questions, you will start to build a stronger foundation for your business idea—one that is rooted in purpose and passion. This foundation will serve as your guiding light through the challenges and triumphs ahead.

The spark that ignited Caruso Valore didn't come overnight, and it wasn't a perfect, neatly packaged idea from the start. It grew through observing my clients, listening to their needs, and aligning those needs with my own values. And that, I believe, is the heart of entrepreneurship: the ability to identify a need, create a solution, and bring it to life in a way that resonates with others.

As you continue this journey, keep your spark close to your heart. Let it be the driving force behind every decision, and trust that it will lead you to something truly meaningful. Your passion, paired with a solid business concept, will become the foundation of something extraordinary.

# Chapter Two

# Chapter Two

## Chapter 2: Foundations of Courage in Launching a Solo Salon

Starting a solo salon was a leap of faith. It meant leaving behind the security of working in someone else's space and taking full responsibility for my own business. There were financial risks, long hours, and doubts. But there was also an incredible sense of freedom and ownership.

I remember the countless hours spent searching for the perfect location. The space needed to be more than just functional—it had to feel welcoming, reflect my style, and align with the experience I wanted to offer my clients. I walked through numerous spaces, envisioning where styling station, and retail displays would go. When I finally found the right spot, it felt like it had been waiting for me all along.

Designing the salon was a labor of love. I wanted it to be an extension of my personality—sophisticated yet approachable, with a focus on comfort and elegance. From choosing the color palette to sourcing furniture that was both stylish and practical, every detail was intentional. The goal was to create a space where clients could relax and feel pampered, a retreat from their busy lives.

Building a loyal clientele was another cornerstone of my journey. This required not only exceptional technical skills but also genuine relationships with my clients. I took the time to listen to their needs, preferences, and even their stories. These connections became the foundation of my business, turning first-time visitors into regulars and regulars into advocates who referred friends and family.

Of course, the path wasn't without challenges. My salon launched just before the COVID-19 pandemic, and the timing brought unprecedented obstacles. The uncertainty of lockdowns, reduced client visits due to health concerns, and the financial strain of maintaining a new business during a global crisis tested every ounce of my resilience.

In those early days of the pandemic, I had to pivot quickly. Implementing rigorous safety protocols, such as enhanced sanitation and spaced-out appointments, became critical to building trust with clients. Communication was key—I kept my clients informed about safety measures through social media and personal messages, reassuring them that their health and comfort were my top priorities.

The financial aspect was one of the most daunting. Securing funding for the salon required careful planning and sacrifices. I had to set a budget for everything—and stick to it. When the pandemic hit, I had to adapt that budget to include unexpected expenses, like personal protective equipment and reduced operating hours. There were moments of doubt, especially when unexpected expenses arose, but I reminded myself that every investment was a step toward realizing my dream.

Time management was another skill I had to master quickly. As the sole owner, I wore many hats—stylist, receptionist, accountant, marketer, and more. During the pandemic, the additional layer of uncertainty meant constantly reassessing priorities and staying flexible. I learned to prioritize tasks, delegate when possible, and set boundaries to ensure I didn't burn out. Scheduling regular breaks and maintaining a work-life balance became essential for sustaining my energy and creativity.

In this chapter, I also want to emphasize the importance of creating a strong brand identity. Your brand is more than just a logo or a name; it's the promise you make to your clients. For me, Studio Di Capelli Salon represents quality, care, and empowerment. I incorporated these values into every aspect of my salon, from the services I offered to the way I engaged with clients on social media. Consistency in messaging and presentation helped establish trust and recognition in a competitive market.

Building relationships with clients wasn't limited to the salon chair. I made it a point to engage with my community, both online and offline. Hosting virtual events, offering promotions, and sharing educational content about hair care allowed me to connect with my audience on a deeper level during a time when in-person interactions were limited. These efforts not only strengthened my client base but also positioned me as a trusted expert in my field.

Another critical aspect of building my solo salon was setting clear goals and tracking progress. I created a business plan that outlined short-term and long-term objectives, from revenue targets to client acquisition goals. Regularly reviewing and adjusting these goals kept me focused and motivated, especially during challenging times like the pandemic.

Lastly, I want to address the emotional journey of starting a solo salon. There were moments of self-doubt when I questioned whether I had made the right decision, especially as the pandemic unfolded. But every time I saw a client's smile or received positive feedback, it reaffirmed my purpose. Surrounding myself with a supportive network of friends, family, and mentors made all the difference. Their encouragement and advice helped me stay resilient and keep moving forward.

This chapter is about more than just the practical steps of building a business; it's about the courage it takes to pursue your dreams, even in the face of the unexpected. Whether you're starting a salon, launching a product line, or chasing a different vision, the principles are the same: stay true to your purpose, be intentional in your actions, and never underestimate the power of persistence.

# Chapter Three

# Chapter Three

**Chapter 3: The Hurdles from Launching a Business during a Pandemic**

Starting a solo salon is never a simple decision, but doing so on the brink of the COVID-19 pandemic added a level of unpredictability that no one could have prepared for. Add to that the shortly thereafter launch of my Caruso Valore Hair and Skin Care line, and I found myself navigating uncharted waters with an incredible amount of pressure—and just as much hope.

This chapter isn't just about my story; it's about the strategies, mindsets, and lessons I learned during one of the most challenging times in modern history. I hope that by sharing these experiences, I can provide a roadmap for anyone facing their own roadblocks, whether in business or in life.

---

### The Vision That Started It All

Launching my salon wasn't just about independence; it was about creating a space that reflected my personal values and professional standards. I envisioned a salon where clients felt pampered, safe, and heard—a space that was more than a place to get your hair done but a sanctuary where self-care was celebrated.

At the same time, my experience as a stylist and my own respiratory challenges (asthma) had ignited a passion for creating natural, high-quality hair and skin care products. I knew the industry needed something fresh, and I felt driven to meet that demand with Caruso Valore.

## Challenges of Launching During a Pandemic

When the pandemic hit, everything changed overnight. Salons were shutting down, product supply chains were disrupted, and fear and uncertainty were at an all-time high. It was terrifying, but I quickly realized that waiting for "better times" wasn't an option. If I was going to succeed, I needed to pivot, adapt, and push forward.

## Strategy #1: Building Resilience by Focusing on Core Values

In the face of uncertainty, I leaned on my core values—quality, safety, and community. This became my North Star, guiding every decision I made for both the salon and my product line. For example:

- **In the Salon:** I implemented rigorous safety protocols to protect my clients and myself. Masks, sanitation stations, and extended time between appointments weren't just compliance measures—they were a promise to my clients that their health and well-being came first. Not to mention this was all state board mandated and new territory for them as well as far as updating guidelines.
- **For Caruso Valore:** I emphasized the natural, health-conscious ingredients in my products, highlighting their benefits for people with sensitive skin or respiratory issues. Messaging focused on self-care during stressful times, which resonated with customers stuck at home.

**Tool for Readers:** Identify your core values and use them as a foundation during times of crisis. Let them guide your decisions and reassure your clients or customers that they can trust you.

---

## Overcoming Financial Hurdles

Starting a business always comes with financial risks, but launching two ventures during a pandemic amplified those challenges. I had to get creative with limited resources and find ways to stretch every dollar.

## Strategy #2: Operating on a Lean Budget

One of the biggest lessons I learned was how to maximize impact with minimal spending. For example:

- **DIY Marketing:** I couldn't afford professional marketing, so I turned to social media. I posted blogs about hair and skin care to keep in touch with clients.
- **Bartering and Collaborations:** I partnered with other small business owners in the community to cross-promote our services and products. This not only expanded my reach but also strengthened my local network.

**Strategy #3: Smart Inventory Management**

When I launched the salon I started with a small product line and focused on high-demand items. By keeping my inventory lean, I was able to manage costs while still offering quality products.

**Tool for Readers:** Create a list of low-cost, high-impact strategies you can use during tough times. Consider areas where you can DIY, collaborate, or focus on essentials.

---

**Building Trust During Uncertain Times**

One of the most difficult parts of launching during the pandemic was earning clients' and customers' trust. Everyone was cautious, and convincing people to step into a salon or try a new product wasn't easy.

**Strategy #4: Transparent Communication**

I made transparency a top priority. I shared every safety measure I implemented in the salon and provided updates on product availability and shipping times for Caruso Valore. My honesty reassured clients that I wasn't just selling services or products—I was genuinely looking out for their well-being.

**Strategy #5: Educating and Engaging**

Instead of focusing on selling, I focused on educating. For example:

- I created content about the importance of self-care during the pandemic, offering tips that included my products but didn't rely solely on them.
- I sent out emails and posted on social media about the steps I was taking to ensure safety and quality, whether that was in the salon or during the product manufacturing process.

**Tool for Readers:** Use transparency and education to build trust. Keep your audience informed and empowered, and they'll become loyal advocates for your business.

---

## Pivoting to Meet New Demands

The pandemic shifted people's priorities, and I had to adapt my business model to meet their evolving needs.

**Strategy #6: Highlighting Versatility**

I tailored my product messaging to emphasize versatility. For example, I showcased how Caruso Valore's Bamboo Sake Hydrating Mist could be used not just as a toner but also as a refreshing midday pick-me-up for people working from home.

**Tool for Readers:** Be flexible and think creatively about how to adapt your offerings to meet your audience's changing needs.

---

**Embracing the Emotional Journey**

Launching a salon and product line during a pandemic wasn't just a professional challenge—it was an emotional rollercoaster. There were days when I felt overwhelmed and questioned whether I could pull it off. But every time a client thanked me for creating a safe space or shared how much they loved my products, it reminded me why I started this journey in the first place.

## Strategy #7: Building a Support Network

I leaned on my husband, daughter, and close friends during the toughest moments. Their encouragement helped me keep going, even when the odds felt stacked against me. I also connected with other small business owners online, sharing experiences and advice that lifted my spirits and gave me new ideas.

## Strategy #8: Prioritizing Self-Care

I learned that I couldn't pour from an empty cup. Establishing daily rituals—like morning meditation, journaling, or simply taking a walk—helped me stay grounded and focused. This wasn't just about surviving; it was about thriving and setting an example for my clients and customers.

**Tool for Readers:** Don't underestimate the power of emotional resilience. Build a support system and prioritize your own well-being to stay strong during tough times.

## Conclusion: Turning Roadblocks into Stepping Stones

Launching a solo salon and a hair and skin care line during the pandemic taught me that roadblocks aren't the end of the road—they're opportunities to grow, adapt, and innovate. The strategies I used—lean budgeting, transparent communication, adaptability, and prioritizing self-care—can help anyone facing challenges in their own journey.

Whether you're launching a business, navigating a personal setback, or simply trying to stay afloat during tough times, remember that you are capable of overcoming obstacles. Lean into your values, stay flexible, and never lose sight of the vision that inspired you in the first place.

But here's the thing—setbacks, whether personal or professional, aren't just roadblocks; they're opportunities to reflect, pivot, and realign. Sometimes, it's about recognizing when it's time to change course, step away from what isn't working, and reimagine your dream. It's not giving up; it's evolving.

For me, this became crystal clear in my journey with Caruso Valore Hair and Skin Care. Deciding to keep the dream alive has been one of the most challenging decisions I've faced. Competing against giants like Amazon and other well-established brands with massive budgets often feels like an uphill battle. Financial hurdles can make you question everything—your path, your vision, and whether you have what it takes to keep going.

There were moments when I wondered if I could make it work, or if I should let it go and move on. But instead of giving up, I used those challenges as a chance to reflect and pivot. I went back to the drawing board—realigning my vision, understanding what my customers truly needed, and figuring out how to stand out in a crowded market. I realized that while I might not have the resources of a big company, I have something they don't: authenticity, a genuine passion for solving problems for my customers, and a personal connection to the brand I've built.

That authenticity is the heartbeat of Caruso Valore, but even with that, I have to constantly evaluate if it's smart to keep going. This isn't about doubt—it's about making educated decisions. Every so often, I step back and ask myself: Is this still the right path? Am I serving my clients the best I can? Is this sustainable for me personally and financially? These are tough questions, but they're necessary. Reflecting on the health of your business and your alignment with its vision isn't about failure; it's about being strategic and intentional about your future.

Reinventing your dream isn't failure—it's resilience. It's about adapting to changing circumstances, evolving your approach, and finding new ways to serve your clients or customers. The journey of Caruso Valore has taught me that success doesn't come from avoiding setbacks but from facing them head-on and refusing to give up on the vision that started it all.

The ability to reflect, adapt, and pivot is what separates those who stagnate from those who thrive. Whether it's reevaluating your product line, rethinking your marketing strategy, or finding new ways to connect with your audience, embracing change is the key to building something sustainable—not just for you, but for the people you're here to serve.

So whether you're picking up the pieces after a setback or simply reevaluating your next step, give yourself the grace to pivot and the courage to dream differently. The solutions you're searching for, both for yourself and for the people you serve, are often waiting on the other side of reinvention. My journey isn't finished,

but if there's one thing I've learned, it's this:
resilience, reflection, and educated decisions
will always carry you forward.

# Chapter Four

# Chapter Four

**Chapter 4: The Setbacks That Built Me**

Every entrepreneur faces setbacks. For me, some of the most difficult moments came from being taken advantage of by others. Whether it was a logistics company that over-promised and under-delivered or marketing consultants who failed to deliver results, these experiences tested my resilience and forced me to adapt.

One particularly painful experience involved a logistics company I hired during a critical phase of my product launch. At the time, I was eager to streamline operations and trusted their promises of reliability and efficiency. However, it quickly became apparent that they were not equipped to handle my business needs. Shipments were delayed, inventory was misplaced, grossly damaged, and customer orders went unfulfilled. The financial impact was severe, and devastating. I remember sitting at my desk, overwhelmed by the financial loss and wondering how I would recover.

In the aftermath, I learned to approach such partnerships with greater caution. I began conducting in-depth research on potential vendors, asking for references, and seeking testimonials from other businesses. I also created a vetting process that included detailed contracts outlining performance expectations and penalties for noncompliance. The experience, though painful, made me a more vigilant and proactive business owner.

Reframing setbacks as opportunities for growth became a vital mindset shift that allowed me to keep moving forward. Initially, setbacks felt like failures, each one chipping away at my confidence. However, over time, I realized that every misstep held valuable lessons that would make me a stronger entrepreneur.

Here's how you can apply this mindset to your own journey:

## Acknowledge and Process the Setback

When faced with a setback, give yourself permission to feel disappointment, frustration, or even anger. Bottling up emotions can make it harder to think clearly. Journaling about what happened or talking it through with a trusted confidant can help you process your feelings and gain perspective.

For example, after the shipping mishap, I took a step back to analyze what went wrong. I acknowledged my own role in the situation—rushing into a contract without thoroughly vetting the company—and committed to learning from the experience. This initial reflection laid the foundation for actionable solutions.

## Shift the Narrative

Reframing is about shifting your internal dialogue. Instead of thinking, "This setback proves I'm not cut out for this," try asking, "What is this situation teaching me?" Viewing challenges as temporary and solvable problems helps you focus on solutions rather than dwelling on the negatives.

For instance, when a marketing consultant failed to deliver results, I initially felt betrayed and discouraged. But reframing the experience helped me realize that it was an opportunity to sharpen my own marketing skills. I took online courses, studied successful campaigns, and gradually became more confident in promoting my brand without relying heavily on outside help.

## Create a Plan of Action

Every setback is an opportunity to develop a new strategy. Ask yourself: What can I do differently next time? How can I prevent this from happening again? Break down your response into actionable steps.

After the shipping debacle, I implemented a checklist for evaluating vendors and established backup plans for critical operations.

## Build Resilience Through a Growth Mindset

Entrepreneurs who view setbacks as stepping stones to success are more likely to persevere. A growth mindset involves embracing challenges, persisting through obstacles, and believing that effort leads to improvement. Celebrate small wins along the way, and remind yourself that every setback is part of a larger journey.

During the pandemic, there were moments when the obstacles felt insurmountable—like when supply chain disruptions delayed the launch of new products, or even getting supplies to stay compliant with new rules and regulations for safety and sanitation... Instead of giving up, I focused on what I could control: improving existing products, engaging with my audience on social media, and brainstorming creative ways to adapt. These efforts not only kept my business afloat but also strengthened my brand's reputation.

## Practical Strategies for Reframing Setbacks

1. Identify the Silver Lining: Look for hidden benefits or opportunities in the situation. A delayed product launch, for example, might give you extra time to refine your marketing strategy.
2. Learn from Others: Seek out stories of successful entrepreneurs who overcame similar challenges. Their experiences can provide inspiration and practical insights.
3. Focus on Solutions: Shift your energy toward brainstorming solutions rather than replaying the problem in your mind. Collaborate with your team or mentors to explore new approaches.
4. Document Lessons Learned: Keep a journal or create a checklist of lessons from each setback. Refer back to these

notes when facing future challenges to avoid repeating mistakes.
5. Practice Self-Compassion: Treat yourself with kindness and understanding. Remember that setbacks are a natural part of the entrepreneurial journey.
6. Build Contingency Plans: Always have a backup plan in place. Whether it's a secondary supplier, an alternative marketing approach, or an emergency fund, preparation can mitigate the impact of setbacks.
7. Seek Feedback: Engage with mentors, peers, or trusted advisors to gain an outside perspective on your challenges. Sometimes, fresh eyes can uncover solutions you may have overlooked.
8. Develop Adaptability: Train yourself to pivot quickly. If one strategy isn't working, be willing to try something new without dwelling on the initial failure.

## Stories of Growth Through Adversity

One of my most significant turning points came when I launched Caruso Valore during the pandemic. Supply chain disruptions, changing consumer behaviors, and the stress of navigating an uncertain market all posed challenges. But these obstacles forced me to innovate. For instance, when in-person events were canceled, I shifted my focus to online marketing and built deeper connections with my audience through virtual engagement.

Another example is the lesson I learned from a failed partnership with a vendor. When the relationship ended abruptly, I felt unprepared to fill the gap. But this experience taught me the importance of maintaining a network of backup suppliers and building stronger communication channels.

## Turning Setbacks Into Strengths

Each setback you encounter as an entrepreneur is an opportunity to build resilience, sharpen your skills, and deepen your understanding of your business. By reframing challenges as opportunities for growth, you not only overcome obstacles but also emerge stronger and more prepared for the future.

This chapter is a reminder that the path to success is rarely linear. The setbacks you face are not roadblocks—they are stepping stones that shape you into a more resourceful, capable, and confident entrepreneur. Embrace them, learn from them, and keep moving forward.

# Chapter Five

# Chapter Five

**Chapter 5: Developing a Resilient Mindset**

Resilience isn't something you're born with; it's something you build. During my journey, I learned to see obstacles as opportunities and to focus on solutions instead of dwelling on problems. This mindset became my greatest tool for navigating the challenges of entrepreneurship, especially during the unpredictable period of launching my solo salon and hair and skin care line during a global pandemic.

**The Importance of Resilience in Entrepreneurship**

Entrepreneurship is inherently unpredictable. From fluctuating markets to unforeseen setbacks, maintaining focus and commitment requires mental toughness. Resilience allows you to bounce back from setbacks, adapt to change, and stay motivated through uncertainty. But resilience isn't just about enduring difficulties—it's about thriving because of them. It's about taking control of your narrative and leveraging challenges as opportunities to grow and innovate.

**Strategies to Cultivate Resilience**

Here are the practices and tools that helped me develop a resilient mindset, which you can incorporate into your own journey:

**1. Embrace the Power of Mindset Shifts**

When I first faced obstacles—like delayed shipments or failed partnerships—it was easy to spiral into negativity. But I realized that my perspective shaped my experience. Instead of labeling these moments as failures, I reframed them as valuable lessons.

**2. Build a Support Network**

Resilience is not a solo endeavor. Surround yourself with people who believe in your vision and can provide guidance, encouragement, or a listening ear. During challenging times, I leaned heavily on my mentors, peers, and even my clients. Their feedback and support reminded me that I wasn't alone in my journey.

Action Step: Join industry-specific groups or forums where you can connect with like-minded entrepreneurs. Attend networking events, even virtually, and actively seek mentorship opportunities.

### 3. Develop a Routine for Mental Clarity

A strong routine can help you stay focused and centered, even during chaos. For me, daily rituals like morning journaling, meditation, became essential. These practices helped me clear my mind, manage stress, and maintain a sense of control.

Action Step: Create a daily routine that prioritizes your mental and physical well-being. Include activities that ground you, such as gratitude journaling or deep breathing exercises.

### 4. Set Clear Goals and Celebrate Small Wins

Big dreams can feel overwhelming, especially when roadblocks appear. Breaking them into smaller, actionable goals can make progress feel more achievable. Celebrating small wins along the way reinforces your commitment and boosts morale.

Action Step: Write down three small, achievable goals each week. Celebrate your progress, no matter how minor it may seem.

## 5. Reframe Failures as Feedback

Every misstep is an opportunity to learn. When a marketing campaign didn't deliver the results I expected, I analyzed the data to understand what went wrong. This experience taught me to test strategies on a smaller scale before committing significant resources.

Action Step: After any setback, reflect on three things you learned from the experience and how you can apply those lessons moving forward.

## 6. Practice Self-Compassion

Entrepreneurship can be unforgiving, but it's crucial to show yourself kindness. During particularly stressful periods, I reminded myself that setbacks don't define me—they're simply part of the process.

Action Step: When faced with a challenge, write down affirmations or positive reminders, such as, "I am capable of overcoming this."

## Tools for Resilience in Your Toolbox

Here are additional tools and techniques to help you build a resilient mindset:

1. Visualization: Spend a few minutes each day visualizing your goals and the steps you need to achieve them. This practice can reinforce your commitment and keep you focused.
2. Gratitude Practice: Reflect on three things you're grateful for daily. Focusing on the positives can help you maintain perspective during tough times.
3. Adaptability Drills: Challenge yourself to step outside your comfort zone regularly. Whether it's trying a new marketing tactic or experimenting with a different product line, building adaptability strengthens your ability to pivot.
4. Emergency Action Plan: Prepare for setbacks by having contingency plans in place. Knowing you have a backup can reduce stress and help you respond quickly.
5. Seek Inspiration: Read books, listen to podcasts, or watch documentaries about other entrepreneurs who have overcome adversity. Their stories can remind you of what's possible.
6. Track Your Growth: Keep a journal documenting how you've navigated past challenges. Revisiting these entries can

provide motivation and clarity when new obstacles arise.

## 7. Turn Setbacks into Experiments

Each obstacle in your journey can become an opportunity to experiment and innovate. For example, when faced with an advertising campaign that failed to generate interest, view it as an experiment. Break down the components—messaging, audience targeting, timing—and refine them for the next attempt.

**Action Step**: After any setback, ask yourself:

- What worked?
- What didn't work?
- What can I test differently next time?

Approaching challenges as experiments removes emotional weight and opens the door to curiosity and improvement.

## 8. Anchor Yourself to Your Why

One of the most powerful motivators during tough times is reconnecting with your core purpose. Why did you start this business? What impact do you want to make? For me, remembering that I launched my solo salon to create a personalized, health-conscious space for my clients kept me moving forward.

**Action Step**: Write down your "why" and place it somewhere visible—on your desk, bathroom mirror, or as a phone wallpaper. When challenges arise, revisit your purpose to ground yourself.

### 9. Invest in Continuous Learning

Adapting to challenges often requires learning new skills or strategies. During the pandemic, I had to immerse myself in online marketing and social media tools. What began as a daunting task soon became a source of empowerment as I realized how these skills elevated my business.

**Action Step**: Identify a skill that could help you overcome a current challenge or grow your business. Dedicate 30 minutes each day to mastering it through courses, books, or online tutorials.

### 10. Create Resilience Rituals

Consistency in your daily rituals fosters resilience. Simple practices, like starting your day with affirmations or ending it by journaling three accomplishments, reinforce your confidence and focus.

**Action Step**: Develop a resilience ritual. For example:

- **Morning**: Write one positive intention for the day.
- **Evening**: Reflect on one challenge you overcame and what you learned.

### 11. Strengthen Your Financial Safety Net

**Fin**ancial setbacks can be one of the most challenging aspects of entrepreneurship. Building a buffer for unexpected expenses or revenue drops allows you to navigate difficult periods with less stress.

**Action Step**: Allocate a portion of your income (If feasible) to an emergency fund. Even small contributions add up over time and provide a sense of security.

### 12. Celebrate Resilience Milestones

**Rec**ognize and reward yourself for enduring and overcoming tough moments. Celebrating these victories—even if they seem small—builds momentum and confidence.

**Action Step**: Create a list of milestones worth celebrating, such as resolving a client conflict or launching a new product despite obstacles. Treat yourself to a reward that aligns with your success.

**Stories of Resilience in Action**

During the pandemic, I faced a particularly challenging moment when in-person sales and hair service clients stopped booking appointments, opportunities disappeared overnight. It forced me to pivot to online platforms, something I had little experience with at the time. I dedicated myself to learning digital marketing strategies, creating engaging social media content, and connecting with my audience in meaningful ways. This pivot not only sustained my business but also opened new avenues for growth.

There was also a time when a major collaboration fell through at the last minute. Instead of succumbing to frustration, I redirected my energy toward smaller, more attainable partnerships. This strategy not only salvaged my momentum but also expanded my network in ways I hadn't anticipated.

## Practical Exercises for Building Resilience

1. Journaling for Clarity: Spend 10 minutes each evening reflecting on the challenges you faced during the day. Write about how you handled them and what you learned.
2. Role-Playing Scenarios: Practice handling hypothetical setbacks with a friend or mentor. Rehearsing your responses can help you feel more prepared when real challenges arise.
3. Mindfulness Training: Incorporate mindfulness exercises, such as deep breathing or guided meditation, into your daily routine. These practices can help you stay calm and focused under pressure.
4. Create a "What If" Plan: Write down potential challenges you might face in your business and brainstorm possible solutions. This proactive approach can reduce anxiety and boost confidence.
5. Daily Visualization Practice: Each morning, close your eyes and visualize yourself overcoming a current challenge and achieving your goals. This mental rehearsal strengthens your belief in your capabilities.

6. Resilience Journal: Maintain a journal where you document each challenge you've faced and how you overcame it. Over time, this serves as a powerful reminder of your strength and adaptability.
7. Accountability Partner: Partner with another entrepreneur to share weekly goals and challenges. Discussing your progress and setbacks can offer fresh perspectives and motivation.

8. **The Logistics Challenge**

Early in my journey, as I discussed earlier, a major logistics company mishandled the delivery and storage of my product line, delaying shipments and damaging product inventory. It wasn't just a logistical nightmare—it also impacted customer trust and was a financial strain. I vowed to prevent this from happening again.

**What I Did**:

1. **Researched Reliable Partners**: I spent time vetting logistics companies,

reading reviews, and consulting other entrepreneurs about their experiences.
2. **Built Redundancies**: I identified backup suppliers and shipping providers to ensure I always had an alternative if one failed.
3. **Communicated Transparently**: I learned that honesty is key. When delays happened, I communicated openly with customers, offering updates and compensation where necessary.

**Lesson for You**: Build systems that mitigate risk, but also be transparent with your clients. People appreciate honesty and effort, even when things go wrong.

### Pivoting to Online Sales

When the pandemic shut down in-person services, I faced a daunting reality: How could I sustain my salon when clients couldn't visit? Instead of succumbing to fear, I used this challenge to explore e-commerce and virtual consultations. I launched a digital storefront for my hair and skin care line..

**What I Did**:

1. **Learned New Tools**: I educated myself on website creation, SEO, and social media marketing.
2. **Engaged Creatively**: I created live tutorials and product demos to connect with clients virtually.
3. **Built Community**: By sharing my journey on social media, I started to foster a loyal online following.

**Lesson for You**: When faced with obstacles, pivot your focus. Look for new ways to serve your audience or expand your reach.

### 1. Resilience Mapping

Create a visual map of your goals, challenges, and potential solutions. For example:

- **Goal**: Launch a new product.
- **Challenge**: Limited budget for marketing.
- **Solution Options**: Leverage social media, collaborate with influencers, create referral programs.

Having this map gives you clarity and a proactive approach to tackling obstacles.

## 2. Stress-Reduction Techniques

Stress can cloud your judgment. Incorporating stress-management practices helps you stay calm and focused:

- **Progressive Muscle Relaxation**: Tighten and relax each muscle group, starting from your toes to your head.
- **Box Breathing**: Inhale for four counts, hold for four counts, exhale for four counts, and repeat.

## 3. Weekly Resilience Check-Ins

Set aside time each week to evaluate your progress and challenges. Ask yourself:

- What went well this week?
- What didn't go as planned?
- What adjustments can I make?

## 4. Mentorship Moments

Schedule regular check-ins with a mentor or accountability partner. Their insights can help you navigate challenges with fresh perspectives.

**5. Vision Board Creation**

Design a vision board that reflects your goals and the resilience you're cultivating. Include inspiring quotes, images, and milestones. Keep it where you'll see it daily as a visual reminder of your purpose.

**Conclusion: Resilience as a Cornerstone of Success**

Resilience isn't about avoiding challenges; it's about embracing them as integral to your growth. By developing a resilient mindset, you'll not only overcome obstacles but also uncover opportunities you never imagined. Remember, every setback is a setup for a comeback. Equip yourself with the tools and strategies in this chapter, and stay committed to your vision, no matter what comes your way.

Resilience isn't just about surviving—it's about thriving. By implementing these strategies and tools, you'll transform challenges into stepping stones for success. Remember, every obstacle you face is an opportunity to grow stronger and smarter. Cultivate resilience, and you'll not only weather the storms but emerge from them more prepared to achieve greatness.

Equip yourself with these practices, and stay steadfast in your pursuit of your vision. Your resilience will not only shape your journey but also inspire others to rise above their own challenges.

# Chapter Six

# Chapter Six

**Chapter 6: The Power of Staying True to Your Vision**

In a world full of distractions, well-meaning advice, and a constant stream of opinions from all directions, staying true to your vision can be incredibly challenging. Whether it's your family, friends, colleagues, or even strangers on social media, criticism and doubt can sometimes feel overwhelming. But one thing is clear: staying aligned with your vision is not only essential—it's powerful. It's the foundation on which your success will be built. So, how do you keep going when the road gets rocky, when others question your decisions, or when your own doubt creeps in?

I've been there. There were countless moments during the early days of launching my business when I felt uncertain, alone, and unsure of the path ahead. But each of these moments provided me with valuable lessons that helped me stay true to my vision. In this chapter, I'm going to walk you through the strategies I used to keep my focus sharp and my mind clear, despite external pressure and internal struggles.

**The Distractions That Will Come**

First, let's recognize the distractions. The world today is louder than ever before. The opinions of others can drown out your own inner voice. It can feel like everyone has an idea of what you should do with your business or your life, and they aren't afraid to share it. I know I've had people tell me that launching a skincare line during a global pandemic wasn't the best idea, or that my vision was unrealistic. Some even questioned the natural ingredients I was so passionate about, doubting whether customers would care about quality over convenience. Or the biggest one, "the market is already saturated."

But here's the truth: whether any of this input is valid or not, it's your vision that matters most. Stay true to your own path, even when others don't see or understand it. Your journey is yours to define, and failure isn't about trying and not making it—it's about never trying at all.

At the same time, part of being true to your vision is recognizing when it's time to pivot—or even walk away. Walking away doesn't have to mean failure. Sometimes, it means having the wisdom to recognize that something no longer aligns with your goals, your values, or the needs of the people you're trying to serve. It means being brave enough to pause, reflect, and make the tough decision to let go in order to create space for something new.

For me, that realization has come up more than once in my journey with Caruso Valore. There were times I questioned if it was smart to keep going, or if I should change direction entirely. But every time, I made the choice to step back, reflect, and make educated decisions. It's not about quitting—it's about evolving. You can reinvent your dream without letting it go entirely. And even if you do walk away, you take the lessons, the growth, and the resilience with you. That's not failure—it's strength.

Every "saturated market" started with someone bold enough to try, and every idea that seemed risky to some became groundbreaking because someone dared to follow through. Trust your instincts, learn as you go, and give yourself the freedom to fail and the courage to pivot. Whether you stay the course, make adjustments, or decide to pursue a completely new path, the key is to always move forward with purpose and intention.

Remember, success isn't about avoiding challenges or never walking away—it's about knowing when to push through, when to shift gears, and when to let go so you can rise stronger. At the end of the day, staying true to yourself and your vision will always be your greatest achievement. Keep going. Failure only happens when you stop learning, and the journey is always worth it.

**The Power of Staying Aligned**

The moment you start doubting yourself or letting the opinions of others take the wheel, you lose sight of the very reason you began this journey in the first place. When I was launching Caruso Valore, I had a singular vision: to create a line of natural, effective products that were good for the body and good for the planet. I knew my products would not only serve my own health needs, but also offer a choice for consumers who were tired of settling for chemical-laden products. My vision was clear, but the path to bringing it to life wasn't.

This is where the power of staying true to your vision becomes undeniable. When your vision is anchored deeply within you, it becomes the compass that guides your decisions. It's not about dismissing criticism or ignoring the obstacles ahead—it's about using that vision as a tool to navigate through the noise.

**Handling Criticism and Doubt**

Now let's dive into the practical side of staying aligned with your vision when faced with criticism and doubt. Below are the steps I've taken to handle these moments, and I encourage you to use them as a guide when you feel your own vision being challenged.

**Step 1: Recognize That Criticism is Part of the Process**

Criticism is inevitable. It comes with the territory of putting yourself and your vision out into the world. Whether it's a customer who doesn't like a product or a colleague who questions your business choices, learning to see criticism as part of the growth process is essential. At first, it may sting. But with practice, you'll learn to separate your personal feelings from the feedback. Is the criticism constructive? Does it come from a place of genuine concern or experience? Or is it just noise?

One of the first things I did when I received negative feedback was to pause. Instead of reacting impulsively, I gave myself time to evaluate the criticism. I asked myself, "Is this helpful? What can I learn from this?" If the feedback was valid and offered an opportunity for growth, I took it to heart. But if it was simply a reflection of someone else's doubts or fears, I let it go.

**Step 2: Separate Emotions from Decisions**

Emotions are powerful, and they can be incredibly useful in helping us connect with our vision on a deeper level. But when it comes to making business decisions, emotions can cloud your judgment and cause you to make choices that don't align with your long-term goals. When I felt myself getting overwhelmed by criticism or doubt, I would take a step back, breathe, and detach from the emotions that were clouding my thoughts.

Instead of reacting immediately to a comment or decision, I gave myself space to assess the situation rationally. This often meant taking a walk, journaling my thoughts, or even talking through my feelings with a trusted mentor. By allowing my emotions to settle, I was able to approach decisions with a clearer, more objective mindset.

**Step 3: Revisit Your Vision**

When you start doubting yourself or feeling overwhelmed by the opinions of others, it's easy to forget why you started in the first place. That's why it's crucial to revisit your vision regularly. Write it down. Post it where you can see it every day. Keep it at the forefront of your mind.

I would often take a moment to revisit my mission for Caruso Valore and remind myself why I chose this path. My vision was bigger than the temporary challenges I was facing. It was about offering people a healthier, more natural alternative in a market flooded with chemicals. It was about creating products I could stand behind with pride. Revisiting that vision helped me push through the hard times and stay aligned with my purpose.

**Step 4: Seek Constructive Support**

When criticism feels like it's too much, seek out a trusted support system. Find people who understand your vision and are willing to give you honest, constructive feedback. This might be a mentor, a business coach, or even a friend who understands the challenges of entrepreneurship.

For me, it was invaluable to have a network of like-minded individuals who could offer perspective when I felt lost. They didn't just tell me what I wanted to hear—they challenged me to think critically about my decisions and helped me stay focused on my vision. Surround yourself with people who will hold you accountable and keep you on track.

**Step 5: Trust Your Instincts**

One of the most important lessons I've learned in my entrepreneurial journey is the power of trusting your instincts. When you're aligned with your vision, your intuition becomes a guiding force. Your gut will tell you when something doesn't feel right, and it will also lead you toward decisions that align with your true purpose.

When I faced moments of uncertainty, I would close my eyes and tune into how a decision made me feel deep down. If it felt aligned with my vision and values, I moved forward with confidence. If it felt off, I trusted that and reevaluated my choices.

## Step 6: Keep the Bigger Picture in Mind

Finally, when you're faced with doubt or criticism, remember the bigger picture. Business and life are long journeys, and you're going to encounter setbacks along the way. What matters is not the setbacks themselves, but how you respond to them. Each obstacle is an opportunity to learn, adapt, and grow.

When I faced moments of self-doubt, I reminded myself that these challenges were just part of the process. I had a clear vision, and with persistence, I knew I could overcome anything standing in my way.

## Conclusion

Staying true to your vision is not always easy, but it's always worth it. When the road gets tough, when others doubt you, and when you feel like the weight of the world is on your shoulders, remember that your vision is your anchor. Use it to guide your decisions, rise above criticism, and stay aligned with your purpose.

Take a deep breath, trust your instincts, and keep moving forward. The world needs your vision, and you're more than capable of making it a reality.

## Digging Deeper into Your Vision for Smarter Decisions

Staying true to your vision while also making smart business decisions is a delicate balance. It's not just about passion or sticking to your guns at all costs—it's about taking the time to evaluate your choices from multiple angles and ensuring that your decisions align with both your personal mission and the demands of the market. To help you navigate this process, here are additional strategies for digging deeper into your vision, evaluating your options, and making educated decisions that honor both your values and your business goals.

## Step 7: Conduct a Vision-Driven SWOT Analysis

One of the most effective ways to evaluate your business decisions while staying true to your vision is by conducting a SWOT analysis (Strengths, Weaknesses, Opportunities, Threats). This analysis allows you to objectively assess your business's current state and make decisions based on facts rather than emotions or external noise.

**How to apply it to your vision:**

- **Strengths**: Consider what strengths your vision brings to the table. What are the unique elements of your product or service that set you apart from competitors? For example, my Caruso Valore line's strength lies in its commitment to natural, eco-friendly ingredients—something I am deeply passionate about. This is a part of my vision, and I know that aligning all business decisions with this strength will help attract customers who value sustainability and quality.
- **Weaknesses**: What challenges or weaknesses might you face that could derail your vision? Are you lacking resources or expertise in certain areas? Knowing these areas upfront allows you to make strategic choices that don't compromise your vision but might require some creativity or external help.
- **Opportunities**: Where do you see opportunities that align with your vision? Perhaps there's a growing trend in your industry that could further

support the products or services you offer. Look for intersections where your vision meets market demand, and use that information to guide smart business decisions.
- **Threats**: What external threats could challenge your vision? Is there competition, market shifts, or economic conditions that may cause disruption? Being aware of these threats allows you to prepare in advance and adapt your strategy without losing sight of your core vision.

By using a SWOT analysis regularly, you can keep yourself grounded in the facts while making decisions that move your business forward in a way that remains true to your purpose.

## Step 8: Align Decisions with Core Values and Long-Term Goals

When faced with a tough decision, ask yourself: *Does this choice align with my core values and long-term goals?* It's easy to get caught up in short-term wins or react impulsively to market trends, but keeping your core values at the forefront ensures you don't stray too far from your true purpose.

For example, one of my core values is sustainability. This has shaped not only my product line but also my sourcing, packaging, and even my partnerships. So, when faced with decisions about working with a potential supplier or entering into a partnership, I always ask myself whether they align with my commitment to sustainability. If they don't, I let that opportunity go—even if it's lucrative. Staying true to my vision isn't just about making money; it's about maintaining integrity.

## Step 9: Perform Market Research, But Stay Authentic

It's essential to research your target audience and keep a finger on the pulse of the market, but that research should always serve to reinforce your vision—not to compromise it. In my case, I knew that people were increasingly looking for natural, non-toxic skin and hair care products. This insight was important, but it didn't sway me toward using chemicals or taking shortcuts to meet the market demand faster.

Instead, I used market research to:

- Validate the demand for the natural ingredients I was already passionate about.
- Find ways to make my products more accessible without losing the integrity of what I stood for.
- Explore trends in the wellness industry that could complement my brand values, such as eco-conscious packaging.

When making business decisions based on research, ensure you are not just reacting to trends but aligning them with the bigger picture of your mission and vision. Your research should back up your beliefs and allow you to adjust intelligently, not abandon your values to follow a trend.

**Step 10: Test Ideas on a Small Scale**

One of the best ways to make educated decisions without risking too much is to test new ideas on a small scale before fully committing to them. This approach allows you to assess the feasibility of an idea while still staying true to your vision.

For example, when I was deciding whether to add a new product to my line, I didn't just jump in. I started with small batches and tested the market with limited quantities. This gave me valuable data on customer demand, pricing, and product feedback, all while maintaining my brand's focus on quality. Testing ideas before fully implementing them allows you to gauge the market's response without losing sight of your core mission.

## Step 11: Stay Connected to Your Customers' Needs

Staying true to your vision doesn't mean ignoring the needs and desires of your customers. It means listening to them and finding ways to serve them while staying aligned with your values. One of the best ways to dig deeper into your vision is to constantly connect with your customer base.

Ask yourself:

- What are their pain points?
- What solutions can you offer that align with your mission?
- How can you continue to innovate while remaining true to your original vision?

It's essential to recognize that your vision may evolve as you learn more about your customers.

For example, as my business grew, I noticed customers were becoming more conscious of the packaging of their products. This led me to explore sustainable packaging solutions that aligned with my mission of reducing environmental impact, while also addressing a growing consumer concern.

## Step 12: Focus on Long-Term Impact, Not Short-Term Results

It's easy to get caught up in chasing immediate results, whether it's a quick sale or a new partnership. But to stay true to your vision, you must focus on the long-term impact of your decisions. Ask yourself: *What is the lasting effect this decision will have on my business, my customers, and the industry?*

By prioritizing the long-term impact of your decisions, you'll not only stay true to your vision but also ensure that your business is built on a strong foundation that supports sustainable growth and success.

---

## Conclusion: Making Educated Decisions with Confidence

In the process of staying true to your vision, remember that you are not making decisions in a vacuum. Your vision, when paired with careful, thoughtful research, self-reflection, and market awareness, is a powerful tool that will guide you through the most challenging moments. The key is to balance emotional attachment with factual analysis, using your deep knowledge of your values and goals to evaluate each choice you face.

Don't be afraid to dig deep into your vision, align your decisions with your core values, and take the necessary steps to ensure that every choice you make propels you toward your long-term goals. By staying true to your vision, making educated decisions, and keeping a clear focus, you will create a foundation for success that will not only stand the test of time but also resonate with your customers and inspire others to follow your lead.

## Step 13: Own Your Decisions and Learn from Mistakes

As an entrepreneur, there will be countless decisions you'll need to make—some big, some small, but all crucial to the success of your business. The reality is that only *you*, the entrepreneur, can make these decisions. You will weigh the pros and cons, analyze the data, and consider the long-term impact, but ultimately, the responsibility falls on your shoulders. No one else can make the call for you, nor should they. Your vision is uniquely yours, and so is the journey that comes with it.

There will be times when you make mistakes. I know I've made plenty. Sometimes, those mistakes will lead to missteps or setbacks. But here's the truth: mistakes are not failures; they are learning opportunities. Every wrong turn is a chance to refine your process, better understand your market, and sharpen your decision-making skills. I remember a time when I misjudged the market demand for a product. The launch didn't go as planned, and I had to pivot. It was frustrating, and it hurt financially. But rather than beating myself up over it, I learned from that mistake and used that experience to better align my future launches with my customers' real needs.

This is why you must own your decisions, both the successes and the failures. Trust that each choice you make, whether it's a win or a loss, teaches you something important. The key is to be open to learning, to remain humble, and to use those lessons to continue moving forward. Your vision will evolve, and your decisions will become more informed, but only through trial, error, and reflection will you gain the clarity and confidence you need to succeed in the long run.

## Step 14: Prioritize Your Physical and Mental Well-Being Along the Way

While it's easy to become consumed by the day-to-day demands of entrepreneurship, it's crucial that you don't neglect the most important asset you have: *yourself*. Building a business is a marathon, not a sprint. If you burn out before you reach your destination, you won't be able to carry out your vision in the way you intended. Taking care of your physical and mental health is essential not just for your well-being, but for the longevity of your business.

As entrepreneurs, we are often so focused on external goals—growth, revenue, market share—that we forget to nurture the internal foundation that keeps us going. When I was starting out, I found myself working 12-hour days, neglecting my health, and dismissing the importance of taking breaks. I thought if I pushed myself harder, I would get ahead faster. But what I realized was that by neglecting my body and mind, I was losing energy, clarity, and the ability to make sharp decisions.

Here are a few ways to prioritize your well-being while navigating the ups and downs of entrepreneurship:

- **Create Boundaries**: It's essential to set clear boundaries between your work and personal life. Set working hours, and make sure you step away from your business when you need to recharge. No matter how much work is on your plate, taking time off will make you more productive in the long run.
- **Stay Active**: Regular physical activity is not just good for your body; it's great for your mind. Whether it's a walk in the morning, yoga, or a full workout routine, moving your body helps to clear your mind, reduce stress, and maintain physical health. I've found that incorporating exercise into my daily routine not only boosts my energy but also helps me stay focused on my goals.
- **Practice Mindfulness**: Mental clarity is just as important as physical energy. Entrepreneurs often juggle multiple tasks and decisions, which can lead to burnout. Practices like meditation, deep

breathing, or even simple mindfulness exercises can help center your thoughts and give you the mental space you need to stay calm and focused.
- **Seek Support**: Don't be afraid to ask for help, whether from a mentor, business coach, or therapist. Having someone to talk to, whether it's to share successes or vent frustrations, can be incredibly grounding. Building a support system around you will make a huge difference when times get tough.
- **Get Enough Rest**: Sleep is a vital component of both physical and mental health. Entrepreneurship can often feel like a never-ending cycle of decisions, meetings, and deadlines. But if you don't rest, you'll run out of fuel. Make sure to get enough sleep, even if it means taking a break from work for the night. Resting allows your mind and body to recover, ensuring you're ready to tackle the next day with fresh energy and a clear perspective.

Entrepreneurship will push you to your limits, but don't forget that your limits are not just about your work ethic. You are a human being, and your vision can only become a reality when you nurture the physical, mental, and emotional well-being that supports it. Taking care of yourself is not a luxury—it's a necessity if you want to sustain the drive and energy required to bring your vision to life.

---

## Conclusion: The Journey is Yours, and Only You Can Lead It

As you navigate the ups and downs of entrepreneurship, remember that staying true to your vision is both a personal and strategic decision. You are the only one who can make the choices that will shape your business and your journey. You will make mistakes, you will face criticism, and you will doubt yourself at times. But with each mistake comes growth. With each challenge, you'll find a deeper understanding of your business and your vision.

Ultimately, it's not just about how well you execute your business plan; it's about the resilience you show in staying true to your purpose through the challenges. By being proactive in learning from mistakes, trusting your intuition, and taking care of your mind and body, you'll create a path that leads to success—not just for your business but for your own well-being along the way.

Wherever your journey takes you, remember that you are in the driver's seat. Stay connected to your vision, trust the process, and never forget to take care of the most important asset on your journey—yourself. The road may not always be smooth, but with a clear vision, a grounded mindset, and a commitment to self-care, you'll build a business that aligns with your purpose and fulfills your greatest potential.

# Chapter Seven

# Chapter Seven

## Chapter 7: Self-Care: The Secret Weapon of Entrepreneurs

As entrepreneurs, it's easy to get swept up in the whirlwind of building and growing our businesses. We work tirelessly to bring our vision to life, often putting ourselves last on the list of priorities. After all, there's always another email to respond to, another task to tackle, another meeting to attend. But here's the truth: no matter how passionate you are about your business, burnout is real, and it's impossible to give your best to your business if you're not taking care of yourself. Your mind, body, and spirit are the foundation of everything you do, and without proper self-care, you'll risk both your well-being and the success of your business.

In this chapter, I want to share personal stories from my journey and explore practical ways to implement self-care—mentally, physically, and emotionally—into your daily life as an entrepreneur. From meditation to Reiki, nutrition to boundaries, self-care isn't just a luxury; it's a necessity that fuels your success.

But along the way, I also encountered my fair share of pitfalls—mistakes that taught me valuable lessons about finding the right balance. This chapter will help you fine-tune your approach to self-care by sharing what worked for me, what didn't, and how you can determine what resonates most with you.

## The Power of Meditation: A Tool for Clarity and Focus

For years, I was caught in the hustle—constantly working, constantly striving, always feeling like I was behind. It wasn't until I started practicing meditation that I realized how much I had been missing out on the power of stillness. Meditation wasn't something I initially believed could help me, but when I gave it a try, I quickly found it to be a game changer.

However, my journey with meditation wasn't without its challenges. The first time I tried to meditate, I struggled to sit still. My thoughts were racing, and I couldn't quiet my mind. It felt like a battle, and I wasn't sure if it was even worth it. I nearly gave up after the first attempt, thinking it wasn't for me. But then, I decided to keep trying and started with just five minutes a day. Slowly, the practice became easier, and I started to feel the calming effects.

There was a time, during an especially overwhelming period of business decisions, where I tried longer meditation sessions, thinking more time would lead to greater benefits. I ended up feeling frustrated and impatient because I couldn't stay focused for the entire duration. I realized that I had set unrealistic expectations for myself. I had to learn that meditation, like any other self-care practice, needs to be adapted to my needs and lifestyle.

**Lesson learned**: Start small, and don't pressure yourself to be perfect. Over time, meditation became a space for me to clear my mind, reduce stress, and reconnect with my vision. I found that just 10-15 minutes in the morning before diving into the day was the sweet spot for me. But for you, it might be different.

What you can take from this: Try different durations of meditation and see what feels right. Don't be discouraged if it takes time to build the habit. Even five minutes of focused breathing can help you reconnect with your purpose.

## Reiki: Energy Healing for Entrepreneurs

Alongside meditation, I've also discovered the benefits of Reiki, a form of energy healing that helps balance the body's energy and promote emotional and physical healing. Reiki is something I initially approached with curiosity, but after my first session, I was hooked.

But there were pitfalls in my journey with Reiki too. Early on, I became very dependent on it to "fix my energy when I felt drained. I was scheduling Reiki sessions weekly, expecting them to instantly heal my emotional and physical exhaustion. However, I eventually realized that while Reiki is incredibly helpful in clearing blockages and bringing balance, it's not a substitute for taking care of myself on a daily basis. It wasn't enough to rely solely on Reiki sessions to "reset" my energy if I wasn't proactively nurturing my body and mind in other ways.

There were also times when I didn't feel immediate relief from a Reiki session, which made me wonder if I was doing it wrong or if I wasn't "open" enough to the energy. I had to remind myself that healing takes time, and every session has its own rhythm. The energy doesn't always work on a conscious level, but rather subtly in the background, shifting your overall state over time.

Lesson learned: Reiki is not all bad—in fact, I am a practitioner myself, and I truly believe in its power and benefits. The key is to use Reiki as a complementary practice to self-care, not as a crutch. Be patient with the process—energy healing works in ways that may not be immediately visible but can be deeply transformative over time. It's a tool that can help you center yourself, release stress, and align your energy, but it works best when paired with other forms of self-care and a proactive approach to your well-being.

What you can take from this: If you're curious about Reiki or energy healing, explore it with an open mind. It's a wonderful practice that can support your journey toward balance and wellness. But don't expect quick fixes—Reiki is most effective when it becomes part of a larger commitment to nurturing yourself, reflecting on your needs, and taking steps to improve your overall health and mindset. Whether you use it as a way to recharge or to deepen your self-awareness, Reiki can be a beautiful addition to your self-care toolbox

## Nourishing Your Body: The Foundation of Self-Care

Physical self-care is just as essential as mental and emotional well-being. The way we fuel our bodies directly impacts our energy levels, mental clarity, and overall performance as entrepreneurs. But as business owners, we often fall into the trap of skipping meals or relying on caffeine and quick snacks to get through the day.

I learned the hard way that this approach wasn't sustainable. There was a time when I'd skip breakfast, grab a coffee on the go, and then barely make time for lunch between meetings and tasks. I constantly felt fatigued, irritable, and unfocused. My productivity was suffering, and my body was sending me signals that something needed to change.

However, when I first tried switching to a healthier diet, I encountered my own set of pitfalls. I went from eating fast food to cooking elaborate meals from scratch, thinking I had to be perfect. I spent hours researching "superfoods" and trying out extreme diets, only to feel overwhelmed by the complexity and the pressure to eat "perfectly." Not to mention I don't like to cook.

Eventually, I learned that self-care in the form of nutrition doesn't need to be complicated. Small, consistent changes—like swapping processed snacks for whole foods or making time for balanced meals—made a huge difference. But I also had to be forgiving of myself. If I had a hectic day and didn't have time to cook a wholesome meal, that was okay. I didn't need to be rigid about it.

*Lesson learned*: Strive for balance and consistency, not perfection. Small steps are better than overwhelming yourself with drastic changes that leave you feeling burnt out.

**What you can take from this**: Start with simple nutrition changes, such as adding more vegetables or drinking more water. Don't be hard on yourself if life gets busy, and try to find a balance that works for your lifestyle.

## Creating Boundaries and Protecting Your Energy

Self-care isn't just about pampering yourself; it's about creating boundaries that protect your energy and mental health. As entrepreneurs, we often feel like we need to say "yes" to everything—to every client, every opportunity, every demand. But overcommitting ourselves can quickly lead to burnout. Learning to say "no" or "not right now" is one of the most powerful acts of self-care you can practice.

I've had to learn this lesson the hard way. Early in my entrepreneurial journey, I was saying yes to every opportunity that came my way, thinking it was necessary for growth. But the constant pressure to do everything left me feeling exhausted and unfulfilled. Eventually, I realized that not every opportunity aligned with my vision, and that it was okay to turn things down that didn't serve my long-term goals.

At first, saying "no" felt uncomfortable. I worried I might disappoint others or miss out on potential opportunities. But I quickly learned that saying "no" was not about rejecting people or experiences—it was about protecting my time, energy, and focus on what truly mattered.

**Lesson learned**: Boundaries are essential for maintaining your energy and focus. Saying no isn't a sign of weakness; it's an act of strength and self-respect.

**What you can take from this**: Start setting clear boundaries around your time. Practice saying "no" when something doesn't align with your goals, and remember that your energy is your most precious resource.

## Conclusion: Fine-Tuning Your Self-Care Strategy

As you continue on your entrepreneurial journey, it's crucial to understand that self-care is not just an afterthought or a luxury reserved for moments when you're feeling overwhelmed. It is the foundation upon which your business and your life are built. You cannot give your best to your business, your family, or your clients if you are not taking the time to nurture your own well-being.

I know that, as entrepreneurs, we are driven. We want to see our businesses thrive, and sometimes, in the pursuit of success, we forget that we are not machines. We are human beings, and we need rest, nourishment, and emotional care to stay strong and capable. At times, I found myself pushing through exhaustion or ignoring the signs my body and mind were sending me. There were moments when I convinced myself that taking a break was a sign of weakness, that I couldn't afford to slow down. But those moments of overwork only led to burnout and a diminished ability to serve my clients or make good decisions for my business.

**Empathy and Motivation: The Entrepreneurial Struggle is Real**

I know you've been there—the pressure of doing it all, feeling like there's never enough time in the day, struggling to balance work with personal life. You may even feel like you're constantly running on empty, wondering if it's even possible to find time for self-care. But let me tell you: it is possible, and it is essential.

You don't have to do it all alone, and you don't have to sacrifice your well-being for the sake of your business. Yes, your dreams are important, but so are you. When you feel like you're at your breaking point, it's okay to pause, reflect, and make adjustments. You are your business's greatest asset, and without a healthy, balanced you, your business can't flourish in the way you've envisioned.

Remember, there is no "perfect" when it comes to self-care. You are allowed to experiment with different techniques, to stumble and learn, and to adjust as you go. What works for someone else may not work for you, and that's perfectly fine. The important thing is to find what makes you feel rejuvenated, recharged, and aligned with your purpose.

**Recap: Your Journey Toward Self-Care**

In this chapter, we've explored several self-care practices that can support your journey as an entrepreneur, including meditation, Reiki, nourishing your body with healthy food, and setting boundaries to protect your energy. I've shared my personal experiences—some of the highs, but also the lows—because I want you to know that you are not alone in this. We all face setbacks, and we all learn along the way. The key is to keep moving forward, knowing that self-care is not just a momentary fix but an ongoing process that supports your personal and professional growth.

1. **Meditation** can be a powerful tool to clear your mind and regain focus, but don't put too much pressure on yourself to "get it right." Start small, be consistent, and let the practice evolve with you.
2. **Reiki and energy healing** can help align your energy and promote healing, but they work best when paired with

proactive self-care. Energy healing isn't a shortcut—it's a supportive practice that works subtly over time.
3. **Nutrition and physical self-care** are the bedrock of your well-being. Avoid extreme diets or complicated routines, and instead focus on making small, sustainable changes that nourish both your body and mind.
4. **Boundaries** are vital. Saying "no" doesn't make you a bad person; it makes you a smart entrepreneur who is protecting your most valuable resource—your energy.

By incorporating these practices into your daily routine, you're not only improving your physical and mental health but also creating the foundation for long-term success. Remember, success isn't just about achieving financial goals or expanding your business. True success is about having the resilience and strength to navigate the ups and downs of entrepreneurship while maintaining your well-being.

**The Bottom Line: Take Care of Yourself, and Success Will Follow**

I want to leave you with this: self-care is not selfish—it's essential. Your business will only be as strong as the person behind it, and that person is you. By honoring your needs and prioritizing self-care, you create a space for yourself to thrive—not only in business but in all areas of life.

As you take your next steps, keep in mind that there will be moments when you feel exhausted, overwhelmed, or uncertain. That's normal. But rather than pushing through these feelings, take a moment to reflect. Reconnect with your self-care practices. Recharge. And remember that you don't have to be perfect. Progress, not perfection, is the goal.

You are capable of achieving everything you've set out to do—and more. But you can only do that when you're at your best, and that begins with taking care of yourself, mentally, physically, and emotionally. The journey may not always be easy, but it will be worth it. Stay aligned with your vision, take time for yourself, and trust that you have everything you need within you to succeed.

And, most importantly, **be kind to yourself along the way.** The road to success is not a sprint—it's a marathon, and your self-care is the fuel that will keep you going, no matter how challenging the journey may seem.

# Chapter Eight

# Chapter 8: Lessons Learned from Being "Taken"

As entrepreneurs, one of the hardest lessons we learn is how to protect ourselves from getting "taken." Whether it's by a service provider, business partner, influencer, or vendor, the sting of being scammed or misled can be painful, both financially and emotionally. I know this from personal experience. Over the years, I've been "taken" more than once—by logistics companies that failed to deliver on promises, influencers who over-promised and under-delivered, media content creators who didn't execute as agreed, and web designers who left me with a half-finished website.

While these experiences were difficult and, at times, even humiliating, they were also transformative. They taught me invaluable lessons about how to safeguard my business, trust my instincts, and, most importantly, how to avoid making the same mistakes again. In this chapter, I'll walk you through some of my stories of getting taken, and more importantly, I'll share the strategies I've developed to help you recognize warning signs, ask the right questions, and protect your business moving forward.

---

## The Pitfalls: Personal Stories of Getting "Taken"

### 1. The Logistics Nightmare: Overpaying for a Promise

I know I keep bringing up the example of the logistics company and the nightmare I experienced, but it was, without a doubt, the most devastating situation I faced at the time. The financial loss, the damage to my brand's reputation, and the emotional toll it took on me as a small business owner made it a defining moment in my journey. The lessons I learned from this experience bear repeating and reiterating in this book, not only to prove a point but also to highlight just how much can be gained from even the most painful setbacks.

As you've read so far, there have been many lessons along the way—moments where things didn't go as planned, where I stumbled, where I trusted the wrong people, or where I had to pivot quickly to recover. But this particular situation was different. It tested my resolve in ways I never expected, forcing me to face the harsh realities of running a business while trying to hold onto the vision and standards I had built my brand on.

The logistics debacle was more than just a bad business relationship. It was a turning point that taught me invaluable lessons about accountability, trust, and the importance of standing up for your brand—even when it feels like the odds are stacked against you. It's an experience I continue to reflect on because the lessons it offered extend far beyond the specific incident.

So, if it feels like I'm harping on this example, it's because I believe its lessons are universal. Whether it's about knowing when to walk away from a toxic partnership, recognizing the signs of poor service before they spiral, or learning how to recover after a significant loss, this story serves as a reminder that even our toughest moments hold value—if we're willing to look for it. And trust me, when you're building something from the ground up, those lessons can make all the difference.

It wasn't until a customer brought to my attention that products they received were broken, incorrect, and not packaged as I had promised—with the designer box, logo tissue paper, and all the little touches to make them feel pampered—that I realized something was terribly wrong. I had been paying a premium for a logistics service that was supposed to deliver an elevated, luxury experience for my customers. Instead, not only were these details neglected, but the situation grew worse when I tried to address it.

When I brought up the issues to the vendor, instead of resolving the problem, the service declined even further. Orders continued to arrive in unacceptable conditions, and customers' trust in my brand was at risk. I finally made the difficult decision to sever the business relationship, hoping to protect the reputation of my company and my vision for Caruso Valore.

Unfortunately, the fallout was devastating. The vendor retaliated by destroying my entire inventory, leading to a significant financial loss that was hard to absorb as a small business owner. It was a painful and costly lesson in trusting the wrong partner, but it taught me the importance of being vigilant, holding others accountable, and advocating for my brand's standards no matter what.

Looking back, the experience was a turning point. It forced me to take a step back, reevaluate my processes, and ultimately learn how to handle logistics on my own. While I'm not yet scaled enough to require a large logistics provider, I've become deeply invested in ensuring every package that leaves my hands reflects the care and quality I promise my customers. From sourcing the right materials to creating a luxurious unboxing experience with designer boxes and logo tissue paper, I've taken ownership of the process to maintain the standards my brand stands for.

This journey has been both humbling and empowering. It reminded me that entrepreneurship often means rolling up your sleeves and doing the work yourself when necessary. It taught me the importance of knowing every aspect of your business—not just to ensure quality, but to build resilience and adaptability as you grow.

Sometimes, setbacks like these aren't just challenges; they're opportunities to refine your craft, learn new skills, and deepen your connection with your customers. While the road has been far from easy, this experience reinforced my commitment to staying true to my vision, delivering excellence, and remaining resourceful no matter the obstacles. It's these lessons that continue to shape my path forward.

.

**Lesson Learned:** Always do your due diligence and seek multiple quotes. Don't just rely on what is promised; ask for references and look for reviews from other businesses who have used the service. Trust your gut—if something feels off, don't ignore the signs. Trusting others to handle important aspects of your business is a big deal, and it's worth taking the time to make sure they are reliable.

---

**2. Influencers and Media Content Creators: The Hype vs. Reality**

Another painful experience came from collaborating with influencers and media content creators to promote my products. Initially, the allure of their large followings and promises of increased exposure seemed like an opportunity I couldn't miss. However, I quickly realized that not all influencers are as invested in your brand as they say they are.

One influencer, in particular, seemed like the perfect fit. They were well-known in my niche, and their engagement rate was impressive. After negotiating a price for a sponsored post and giving them free product samples, I was eager to see the results. I watched as the post went live, but soon realized it lacked the depth and enthusiasm I had hoped for. The influencer barely mentioned my brand, and the link to my store wasn't even included in their bio as promised. There was little to no engagement, and the return on investment was non-existent. Worse, when I reached out to ask for feedback or an update, I received no response.

This experience left me feeling disillusioned with influencer marketing and questioning if I was just another person buying into the hype. I had placed my trust in this influencer's reputation, but I hadn't fully understood their level of engagement or how much effort they would truly put into my campaign. At the time, I didn't ask the right questions about their audience, how they engage with their followers, or their past experiences working with brands.

**Lesson Learned:** When collaborating with influencers or content creators, be specific about deliverables, timelines, and expectations. Don't rely solely on their promises—get everything in writing. If an influencer claims to have a certain reach or engagement, ask for proof before agreeing to terms. Be clear about your goals and the results you expect. If they're serious about working with you, they should be equally committed to meeting the terms of the agreement and providing evidence of their work.

---

**3. Web Designers: The Half-Done Website**

One of the biggest financial missteps I made early on was hiring a web hosting service that required a large upfront payment with promises of a fully customized, professional website for my business. I wanted a site that aligned with my vision—elegant, user-friendly, and reflective of my brand. Initially, everything seemed straightforward, and the company's portfolio appeared impressive. But once the payment was made, things quickly began to unravel.

The platform they built was difficult to navigate, with no clear guidance on how to make updates or changes myself without paying additional fees for every minor adjustment. Communication became a nightmare—customer service was slow, unhelpful, and often nonexistent when I needed critical support. What I ended up with was a site that fell far short of expectations, was riddled with issues, and left me feeling stuck with a service that wasn't delivering on its promises.

This experience was a hard pill to swallow, but it taught me a valuable lesson: Always do your research, not just on the cost or the product, but on the long-term usability and support that comes with it. Today, I manage my website myself. While it's not as glamorous as outsourcing to an expensive provider, I've learned how to create and maintain a site that meets my needs without the headaches of relying on someone else.

This experience reinforced an important entrepreneurial truth: You don't have to outsource everything to succeed, and sometimes the best solutions come from learning to do it yourself. It's not always ideal, but it's empowering to know you're in control and able to pivot when needed. Challenges like these remind us that setbacks aren't failures—they're opportunities to grow, adapt, and ultimately come back stronger.

**Lesson Learned:** When hiring anyone—whether it's a web designer, contractor, or any service provider—make sure you're clear about deliverables and deadlines. Break the project down into milestones with agreed-upon payment schedules. If they fail to meet any deadlines, you should have the right to stop payment. Always check their previous work and ask for references. A good designer should have a portfolio with successful case studies that demonstrate their ability to meet your specific needs.

---

### 4. The Overzealous Social Media Marketer

Finally, there was the social media marketing agency that promised to take my brand to the next level. I was in over my head and figured outsourcing my social media management would free up time to focus on other areas of my business. They sold me on the idea of increased visibility and engagement, but after months of paying for their services, my followers remained stagnant, and my engagement was lower than ever.

When I asked for reports on the work they had been doing, they gave vague answers and no concrete data. I realized I had been paying for services that were either not being rendered or weren't effective in the way I had hoped. I didn't see the results, and the money spent on this agency felt like an expensive lesson in marketing.

**Lesson Learned:** Before hiring a marketing agency or any consultant, ask for case studies and reports from other clients they've worked with. Don't just take their word for it. And, as always, have clear expectations and agreements in writing, particularly with measurable outcomes. Ask for regular updates on campaigns, and always question anything that seems vague or unfocused.

---

## Building a Safeguard Strategy: Protecting Your Business

Through these painful experiences, I've learned the importance of safeguarding my business against being taken advantage of. Below are the strategies I now use to protect myself, and that I highly recommend you implement as well.

## 1. Do Thorough Research and Vetting

Before hiring anyone, whether it's a logistics company, influencer, web designer, or marketing agency, take the time to do your research. Look for online reviews, ask for recommendations, and don't hesitate to check out their portfolio or previous work. It's also important to ask other business owners about their experiences with the service provider. One of the biggest mistakes I made was rushing into agreements without doing enough background checks. Trust me, taking a few extra hours to research can save you weeks—or even months—of frustration.

Start by compiling a list of potential service providers and do a deep dive into their reputation. Look for complaints or red flags, but also note positive reviews and success stories. Reach out to other business owners who have used them, and ask for honest feedback about their experiences. It's easy to get swept up in the excitement of scaling, but taking time to research thoroughly is one of the best ways to avoid mistakes.

## 2. Always Have a Contract

A contract is your best protection. While it may feel uncomfortable to negotiate terms in writing, it is essential for setting clear expectations. Every agreement should outline the scope of work, deliverables, timelines, payment terms, and penalties for not meeting deadlines. Even if you are working with someone you trust, having a written agreement protects both parties and ensures that everyone is on the same page. If an issue arises, a contract gives you a legal basis to resolve the matter.

Make sure the contract clearly outlines milestones and deadlines, with provisions for what happens if things go off course. Always take time to review the terms carefully and don't be afraid to negotiate changes that better align with your needs. If a service provider is unwilling to put things in writing, that's a major red flag.

---

## 3. Ask the Right Questions and Trust Your Gut

The most important lesson from these experiences was learning to trust my instincts.

If something doesn't feel right, it probably isn't. Don't ignore your gut feeling when something feels off during a negotiation or after an initial interaction. Ask tough questions and dig deeper into how they plan to execute on their promises. Asking the right questions isn't just about making sure the provider can do the job—it's about understanding how they will meet your expectations.

The more you understand what's involved and what to expect, the less likely you'll be taken advantage of. Inquire about their process, ask for data or references, and make sure you fully understand how they'll deliver on their promises. If their answers are vague or they avoid specifics, be cautious.

---

By understanding the potential pitfalls and having the right strategies in place, you can protect yourself from being "taken." Keep these lessons in mind as you navigate your entrepreneurial journey, and always remember that the best way to avoid being scammed is to be proactive, educated, and always trust your instincts.

## Recognizing Scams in Emails and Snail Mail: Protecting Yourself from Unnecessary Charges and Scare Tactics

As an entrepreneur, part of safeguarding your business involves being vigilant not just about your partnerships, but also about unsolicited communications you might receive—both digitally and via traditional mail. Scammers, marketers, and unscrupulous solicitors are constantly looking for opportunities to target businesses, often using scare tactics or false promises to try to separate you from your hard-earned money.

It's easy to overlook seemingly benign emails or letters, but if you're not careful, you could be falling victim to a scam or paying for services that you don't actually need. In this section, I'll help you recognize warning signs in both emails and snail mail, and share strategies for vetting these communications so you can make informed decisions before responding or paying any fees.

**Spotting Scam Emails: Red Flags to Watch For**

Scam emails are one of the most common ways businesses get tricked into paying for services they don't need or even falling for a full-on scam. The key to avoiding these fraudulent attempts is being able to quickly identify the warning signs. Here's how to recognize them:

**1. Generic Greetings and Lack of Personalization**

One of the first red flags you might notice in a scam email is the lack of personalization. If the email begins with a vague "Dear Business Owner" or "Dear Customer," instead of addressing you or your business by name, this is an immediate warning sign. Scammers often send mass emails to hundreds or even thousands of people, hoping to catch someone who will fall for their bait. A legitimate company that's reaching out to you will almost always address you by name or reference something specific to your business.

**2. Urgent Language or Threats of Consequences**

Scam emails often use urgent language or threats to create a sense of fear, such as, "Your business is at risk," "Immediate action required," or "Failure to respond will result in legal action." They want you to make a rushed decision without taking the time to think clearly or research what they're asking. These emails may even claim to be from government agencies, lawyers, or regulatory bodies, trying to intimidate you into taking immediate action.

**Example:** You might receive an email claiming your website has been reported for copyright infringement or that you owe a fine, and if you don't act within 24 hours, you'll face a significant penalty. These types of emails are often not legitimate and are meant to scare you into paying money to avoid a "disaster."

### 3. Suspicious or Unknown Sender

Look at the sender's email address closely. Scammers often disguise their email addresses to appear legitimate, such as "support@paypal.com" or "invoices@yourbank.com." However, if you hover over the email address or look at the domain closely, you may notice it's not a genuine email address. For example, instead of "paypal.com," it could read something like "paypal.support@xyzmail.com." Always double-check the domain of the sender's email address to ensure it matches the legitimate source they claim to represent.

## 4. Unsolicited Requests for Money or Personal Information

Any email requesting payment upfront or asking for sensitive business information—like your banking details, tax ID number, or login credentials—should be regarded with suspicion. Legitimate companies will not ask you for this kind of information via email. If the sender is pressuring you to provide personal or financial details, it's best to avoid engaging with them and report the message as spam.

## 5. Spelling and Grammar Mistakes

While a typo or two may happen in legitimate emails, multiple spelling and grammar mistakes are often a red flag that the email is from a scammer. Fraudulent companies don't always take the time to proofread their messages, and these errors can be easy to spot.

### Safeguard Strategy for Email Scams:

- If you receive a suspicious email, do not click on any links or open any attachments. Instead, go directly to the official website of the company or organization that supposedly sent the message to verify the claim.

- Use tools like Google or other search engines to search for keywords from the email—such as the sender's email address or the claims made in the message—to see if other businesses have reported similar scams.
- Always verify any request for payment or sensitive information. Call the company or organization directly using a phone number from their official website—not one provided in the email—to confirm if they actually contacted you.

**Recognizing Scam Snail Mail: Tactics to Avoid Falling for Fraudulent Offers**

While scam emails are common, don't overlook the possibility of fraud through traditional mail. Scammers have perfected the art of creating convincing letters that appear official or even urgent. These letters can come from all sorts of sources—"government agencies," "business support organizations," or "industry experts" claiming that you need to make a payment for a service you didn't request. Here's how to spot them:

**1. Official-Looking but Vague Language**

Scam letters often look highly official, with professional-looking logos, watermarks, and legal jargon designed to trick you into thinking they're from a legitimate source. However, if you take a closer look at the language, you'll notice it's vague or misleading. The letter might demand payment for a "special certificate" or "required compliance" without ever fully explaining what the service is or why it's necessary for your business.

**Example:** You might receive a letter claiming that your business is not in compliance with local regulations and that you need to pay an urgent fine to avoid penalties. The letter may even include an official-looking form to fill out with your business's details.

**2. Requests for Unnecessary Fees**

Scam letters often focus on offering services that you don't need or that are unnecessary. They might offer to register your business with a government database or create a trademark for you for an inflated fee. The problem is that many of these services are either free or available for far less through official channels.

**Example:** You might get an official-looking letter about "Domain Name Registration" or

"Annual Business Compliance" that instructs you to pay a fee for services that are already taken care of by government agencies or that don't need to be renewed at all.

## 3. Lack of Contact Information or Valid References

A legitimate business will provide clear contact information, including a physical address and a working phone number. Scam letters often lack these details or use vague contact information. Always verify the company's identity by checking online reviews, business directories, or official government websites before responding.

## 4. Unsolicited Offers for Business Services

Be wary of any unsolicited letters that offer "exclusive deals" or "special services" for a fee. Many of these letters are designed to make you feel like you've been selected for a limited-time offer, creating a sense of urgency. The key here is to remain calm and skeptical—there is no rush to pay for services you haven't requested.

**Safeguard Strategy for Snail Mail Scams:**

- Don't act on any letter that makes urgent or threatening claims, such as fines or penalties. Take time to research and verify the authenticity of the letter before making any payments.
- Look for any mention of official-sounding fees or services that are already provided for free or at a low cost by government entities or industry organizations. Always check with the legitimate sources before committing to any offer.
- Check the sender's contact details. Call them using official numbers from their website (never those listed on the letter) to verify if they sent the communication.
- If the letter requests payment for something like a business listing or government service, visit the official government or industry website to check if this is a legitimate request.

## Create a Scam-Vetting System for Your Business

To protect your business, create a safeguard strategy that includes a "scam vetting system" for emails, snail mail, and phone calls. Here's how to implement it:

1. **Develop a Checklist for Scrutinizing Communications:**
    - Is the communication personalized or vague?
    - Does it include urgent language or scare tactics?
    - Are the contact details legitimate and traceable?
    - Is the service being offered necessary or redundant?
    - Does the price align with industry standards?
2. **Create a Response Protocol:**
    - **Step 1:** Review the communication critically. If it feels rushed or suspicious, stop and research before responding.
    - **Step 2:** Verify claims by contacting the company or organization using trusted contact details, not those provided in the letter or email.
    - **Step 3:** Ask for references or case studies if they claim to have

served other businesses in your industry.
- **Step 4:** If the communication offers services for a fee, research the necessity and legitimacy of these services before making any payments.
3. **Educate Your Team and Stakeholders:**
   - Share the warning signs and vetting strategies with anyone who handles business communications, so everyone knows what to look for and can act quickly to stop potential scams.

By staying vigilant and following these steps, you can protect your business from unnecessary costs and fraudulent practices. Remember, scams can come in many forms—always trust your instincts and never make hasty decisions.

# Chapter Nine

# Chapter Nine

## Chapter 9: Reflecting on Success and Reframing Failure

Success and failure are two sides of the same coin, intricately linked in the journey of any entrepreneur. While society often celebrates the visible rewards of success, it is the hidden struggles, lessons, and resilience born from failure that truly shape who we are.

For me, success is deeply personal—it isn't just about the numbers in my bank account or the accolades on my wall. It's about the sense of purpose I feel in creating something meaningful, the relationships I've built, and the growth I've experienced along the way. This chapter will delve deeper into what success really means, how to use failure as a stepping stone for greater achievements, and how my personal stories of setbacks—ranging from navigating the COVID-19 pandemic to overcoming scams—can inspire and guide you to stay focused and committed to your own vision.

## Defining Success on Your Own Terms

Success is unique to every individual. It's not a one-size-fits-all concept, and chasing someone else's version of success can leave you feeling unfulfilled. Early in my career, I believed success was solely about achieving financial independence and stability. But as I launched my salon and product line, my definition evolved. I realized that success wasn't just about building financial security or creating future retirement income—it was also about making an impact. Empowering my clients to feel confident in their skin, solving their needs with thoughtful solutions, and offering safe, natural products in a market saturated with artificial options became just as important as the numbers on a balance sheet.

For me, success became a balance between financial growth, future security, and staying true to my vision of serving others. It's about creating value not just for myself but for my clients—truly listening to their needs, solving their problems, and building something sustainable that continues to make a difference over time. Success is not about fitting into a mold but about crafting a life and business that align with your values, your goals, and the impact you want to leave behind.

For you, success might mean freedom, the ability to spend more time with your family, making a difference in your community, or simply waking up every day excited about what you do. The key is to align your goals with your values and passions. When your definition of success resonates with your core beliefs, it becomes a powerful motivator that propels you forward.

**Reflective Exercise: Defining Success**
Take some time to reflect on what success means to you. Answer the following questions in your journal:

- What does success look like in your personal life?
- What does success look like in your professional life?
- How do your goals align with your values and passions?
- What would you feel, see, or experience when you achieve your version of success?

## Using Failure as a Stepping Stone

No entrepreneur escapes failure. It's not a matter of "if" you'll face setbacks but "when." The difference between those who thrive and those who give up is the ability to reframe failure as an opportunity to learn and grow. Every failure holds a lesson, and every lesson is a stepping stone toward greater achievements.

### The Financial and Emotional Toll of Missteps

When I invested in a TV commercial and a magazine ad that promised to bring massive exposure to my brand, the financial loss was significant, but the emotional toll was even greater. The campaigns came with bold promises of airing in specific markets and reaching a broad audience. However, once I paid the "talent," the communication all but disappeared. There was no transparency or proof that the ads ever aired where they claimed, and the results were such a disappointment—virtually no engagement or increase in sales.

It was disheartening to realize that I had poured so much time, money, and trust into what felt like a perfect opportunity, only to be left with nothing to show for it. The lack of accountability from the vendors and the inability to verify the work made me feel like I had been taken advantage of.

That experience forced me to take a step back and reevaluate how I approached marketing decisions. I learned the importance of asking tough questions, demanding accountability, and ensuring that every strategy aligns with my brand and audience. It was a hard but valuable lesson in staying vigilant and strategic, reminding me that not every shiny opportunity is worth the cost.

From that moment on, I established stricter vetting processes. Now, I ask for referrals, conduct in-depth research on potential partners, and trust my instincts when something feels off. This process, while time-consuming, has saved me from making similar costly mistakes in the future.

**Action Step: Build a Partnership Vetting Process**

Create a checklist for evaluating potential partners. Include these steps:

1. **Research**: Check reviews, ratings, and the company's track record.

2. **Referrals**: Request testimonials or references from previous clients.
3. **Contracts**: Ensure all terms are documented clearly in writing.
4. **Trial Period**: Start with a small project to test reliability.
5. **Instinct Check**: If something feels wrong, investigate further or walk away.

---

**Lessons from the Pandemic: Pivoting with Purpose**

The COVID-19 pandemic was a global setback, but for me, it was also a wake-up call. Overnight, the traditional salon model became unsustainable. At First we were shut down, and even after re-opening clients canceled appointments, and physical retail spaces became inaccessible. I utilized the downtime to learn new skills—not only to enhance my hair services but also to strengthen the behind-the-scenes operations of my business.

I shifted my focus online, building an e-commerce platform for my product line and investing in digital marketing courses. I learned how to use social media to maintain connections with my clients and expand my reach. The experience showed me the importance of adaptability and using unexpected challenges as a chance to grow. While the pandemic tested every aspect of my business, it ultimately strengthened my foundation and gave me the tools to thrive in ways I hadn't anticipated.

**Action Step: Prepare for Uncertainty**
Think about how you can diversify your business to withstand future challenges:

1. Identify alternative revenue streams (e.g., online sales, digital products, virtual services).
2. Build a digital presence to connect with clients anytime, anywhere.
3. Develop contingency plans for potential disruptions.

---

**Celebrating Small Wins**

In the chaos of setbacks, it's easy to overlook progress. Early in my career, I made the mistake of only celebrating major milestones. But as I faced challenges, I realized the importance of acknowledging even the smallest victories—whether it was a single glowing customer review or successfully meeting a production deadline.

Celebrating small wins not only keeps you motivated but also reminds you of how far you've come. It shifts your focus from what went wrong to what you've accomplished.

**Action Step: Create a Win Journal**
Keep a journal where you record daily or weekly wins. Reflect on what you did to achieve them and how they contribute to your larger goals.

---

## Turning Setbacks into Opportunities

Every setback I've faced has taught me something invaluable. Whether it was refining my business processes, learning to communicate more effectively with customers, or finding innovative solutions to unexpected challenges, these lessons have shaped me into a stronger entrepreneur.

**My 5-Step Framework for Turning Setbacks into Growth:**

1. **Pause and Reflect**: Allow yourself to feel disappointed, but don't dwell on it. Take a step back to assess the situation objectively.
2. **Identify the Lesson**: Ask yourself, "What can I learn from this experience?"
3. **Adjust Your Approach**: Use the lessons to refine your strategies and processes.
4. **Take Action**: Develop a plan to move forward, incorporating what you've learned.
5. **Celebrate the Growth**: Recognize the strength and wisdom you've gained from overcoming the challenge.

---

## Interactive Worksheet: Redefining Success and Reframing Failure

### Exercise 1: Your Definition of Success

- List three goals you've achieved that make you feel proud.

- Reflect on what those achievements taught you about yourself.

**Exercise 2: Reframing a Setback**

- Write about a recent failure or challenge.
- What lessons did you learn?
- How can you use those lessons to improve your approach moving forward?

**Exercise 3: Vision Mapping**

- Create a mind map of your definition of success. Include personal, professional, and financial goals, as well as values and passions.

**Checklist: Building Resilience**

1. Start a daily gratitude practice.
2. Surround yourself with supportive people.
3. Develop a personal mantra to repeat during tough times.
4. Regularly review and adjust your goals.
5. Celebrate small wins and milestones.

## My Final Reflections on Success and Failure

The lessons I've learned through setbacks have been some of the most valuable in my journey. If I hadn't faced roadblocks like the pandemic, scams, and getting "taken", I wouldn't have discovered my own resilience or built the skills that now define my business.

When I look back at the challenges I've faced, it's clear that success isn't about avoiding failure—it's about embracing it, learning from it, and using it as a springboard for greater achievements. Your setbacks don't define you; they refine you. Every disappointment, every closed door, and every unexpected twist has played a crucial role in shaping my entrepreneurial journey. It's through these moments that I've learned the most about myself, my business, and the importance of perseverance.

One of the most transformative lessons I've learned is that failure forces us to look inward. It strips away the external markers of success and makes us confront the core of who we are and why we do what we do. For me, those moments of reflection often led to breakthroughs. When a product arrived broken or not at all,, I initially felt panic and frustration. But after stepping back and reflecting on the situation, I realized that this was an opportunity to communicate openly with my customers and show them the human side of my brand. That single shift in mindset turned a potential failure into an opportunity to build trust and loyalty with my audience.

Another pivotal realization was understanding that success is not a destination but a journey. This mindset shift has been liberating. For so long, I thought success would be a specific milestone—reaching a certain revenue number, getting featured in a magazine, or expanding my product line to a set number of stores. But as I achieved some of these goals, I realized that the satisfaction they brought was fleeting. The true joy came from the process of working toward them—the late nights brainstorming new ideas, the excitement of launching a new product, and the sense of pride in overcoming obstacles along the way.

The idea of redefining success has also been crucial in maintaining my motivation and focus. In the early stages of my business, I often compared my progress to others. It's easy to fall into the trap of measuring your worth against someone else's highlight reel. But the truth is, everyone's journey is unique. What works for one person may not work for another. Once I stopped comparing myself to others and started focusing on my own definition of success, I found a sense of peace and clarity. Success, for me, is about creating something that aligns with my values, serves my clients, and brings fulfillment to my life. It's about the small, meaningful moments—like a customer sharing how my product or service has improved their hair or skin or a client telling me they feel confident and beautiful after visiting my salon.

Another important lesson I've learned is the value of resilience. Resilience isn't just about bouncing back from setbacks; it's about growing stronger because of them. Each challenge I've faced has taught me something new—whether it's the importance of vetting suppliers, the power of clear communication, or the need to stay adaptable in an ever-changing business landscape. These lessons have become the foundation of my business, guiding my decisions and helping me navigate future challenges with confidence.

I've also come to understand that failure is an essential part of innovation. When I first started my business, I was so afraid of failing that I often played it safe. But over time, I realized that some of my biggest breakthroughs came from taking risks and trying new things, even if they didn't always work out.

Another aspect of failure that's often overlooked is its ability to foster empathy and connection. When you've experienced setbacks, you're better able to relate to others who are going through similar struggles. This has been particularly meaningful in my interactions with other entrepreneurs. Sharing my story of launching during a pandemic, dealing with scams, and navigating vendors not living up to their end of the business dealings, and financial losses, has allowed me to connect with others on a deeper level. It's a reminder that none of us are alone in our struggles and that there's strength in community and collaboration.

Reflecting on these experiences, I've also come to appreciate the importance of celebrating progress—no matter how small. In the early days of my business, I often overlooked small wins because I was so focused on the bigger picture. But over time, I've learned that those small victories are what keep you going.

Whether it's completing a challenging task, receiving positive feedback from a customer, or simply making it through a tough day, each step forward is worth celebrating. These moments of recognition remind me of how far I've come and motivate me to keep pushing forward.

One of the most valuable tools I've discovered in navigating both success and failure is the power of reflection. Taking the time to pause, evaluate, and learn from my experiences has been transformative. I've made it a habit to regularly review my goals, assess what's working, and identify areas for improvement. This practice has not only helped me stay focused but also allowed me to approach challenges with a clearer perspective.

Finally, I want to emphasize the importance of staying true to yourself. In the business world, it's easy to get caught up in trends, competition, and external pressures. But at the end of the day, your authenticity is what sets you apart. Every decision I've made—from the ingredients I use in my products to the way I communicate with my clients—has been guided by my values and vision. Staying true to myself has not only helped me build a business I'm proud of but also allowed me to connect with customers and clients on a genuine level.

So, what does all of this mean for you? It means that no matter where you are on your journey, you have the power to define your own success. You have the ability to turn setbacks into opportunities, to learn and grow from every challenge, and to create a life and business that aligns with your values. It means that failure isn't something to fear but something to embrace as a natural and necessary part of the process.

As you reflect on your own journey, remember that success is not a straight line. It's a winding path filled with ups and downs, detours and surprises. But each step—whether it feels like a leap forward or a stumble back—brings you closer to your vision. Trust the process, believe in your resilience, and never underestimate the power of your determination.

In the end, success isn't about avoiding failure; it's about learning from it, growing because of it, and continuing to move forward despite it. Your setbacks don't define you—they refine you. They shape you into a stronger, wiser, and more capable version of yourself.

So, keep going. Celebrate your progress, embrace your challenges, and stay true to your vision. Every twist and turn is a part of the adventure, and every step forward—no matter how small—brings you closer to your goals. Success is not a destination; it's a journey, and you're already on your way.

# Chapter Ten

# Chapter Ten

## Chapter 10: Staying Inspired and Motivated Through Challenges

Life as an entrepreneur is filled with unexpected twists and turns. There are high points and low points, moments of triumph and moments of doubt. Yet, what makes the difference between success and failure is the ability to stay motivated, especially through the inevitable challenges that arise. For me, the journey wasn't just about overcoming business hurdles—it was also deeply intertwined with my personal health struggles. These challenges shaped my vision and ultimately became the driving force behind the creation of Caruso Valore. Every obstacle was a stepping stone that pushed me to persevere, to innovate, and to create something that would not only improve my life but also the lives of others.

## A Personal Turning Point: Battling Respiratory Issues

Before Caruso Valore was even a thought, my life was marked by ongoing health struggles. Asthma and other respiratory issues consumed much of my energy. On many days, even the simplest of tasks felt monumental. Breathing difficulties were not only physically exhausting but also emotionally draining. I would find myself feeling discouraged, searching for any relief, and feeling trapped in a cycle of doctor visits, medications, and treatments that seemed to offer no permanent solution.

The emotional toll of struggling with my health was significant. It wasn't just the frustration of not feeling well—it was the feeling of being limited by my own body. Simple activities like taking a walk, visiting a store, or even being around certain scents would trigger my symptoms. Over time, I became hyper-aware of the products I was using in my environment. I began to realize that many of the daily products I used were loaded with harsh chemicals and artificial ingredients, things that could exacerbate my condition rather than help it. I wondered: Could there be an alternative? Could I create something that would not only help me but also help others?

This question would lead me on a journey of discovery, one that would eventually shape the creation of Caruso Valore.

**The Birth of Caruso Valore**

Caruso Valore was born out of a personal journey rooted in necessity, passion, and health. As a stylist and someone who has long struggled with respiratory issues, I became increasingly aware of how artificial additives and overpowering chemicals in mainstream products were affecting not only my clients but my own well-being. The constant exposure to these irritants made it clear that I needed to make a change—not just for myself, but for others who faced similar challenges.

I envisioned a product line that would complement the salon experience while also prioritizing health and mindfulness. I wanted to create something that enhanced the professional care clients received in the salon and allowed them to extend that care into their daily routines—without sacrificing their health. The goal wasn't simply to create beauty products but to solve a deeper issue: offering effective, high-quality solutions that were safe for both the body and the environment.

This personal challenge became my purpose. I set out to design products that I could feel proud to recommend—free of harmful chemicals, gentle on sensitive systems, and supportive of self-care. Caruso Valore became more than just a product line; it was a mission to fill a gap in the market and provide others with the same relief and confidence I sought for myself.

For anyone on an entrepreneurial journey, I encourage you to think deeply about your "why." What problem do you want to solve? What passion drives you to create? My respiratory struggles gave me clarity about the kind of change I wanted to make, and it became the foundation for Caruso Valore. When you let your challenges guide your purpose, you can create something truly meaningful—something that not only aligns with your values but also makes a real difference for others.

**Finding Inspiration in Challenges**

Building a business is never a smooth journey. Along the way, there were many moments when I doubted myself and questioned whether I was doing the right thing. The challenges were overwhelming at times. But despite these obstacles, I found ways to stay motivated. The key was to embrace the challenges as part of the journey, rather than viewing them as insurmountable roadblocks.

Here are some of the strategies that helped me stay inspired and motivated throughout the difficult moments:

**1. Embracing a Growth Mindset**

One of the most important lessons I learned throughout my entrepreneurial journey was the power of a growth mindset. I realized that every challenge presented an opportunity to learn, grow, and refine my approach. It was easy to become frustrated when things didn't go as planned, but rather than letting that frustration hold me back, I started viewing setbacks as opportunities to improve. Whether it was learning from a mistake, gaining new skills, or rethinking my strategy, each challenge became an essential part of my growth as an entrepreneur.

Instead of focusing on the obstacles, I learned to focus on the lessons that each challenge brought. This shift in perspective made all the difference in how I approached problems.

**2. Surrounding Myself with Positivity**

The people around you have an incredible influence on your mindset and motivation. Throughout my journey, I made it a point to surround myself with positive, supportive individuals who encouraged me to keep going even when things felt tough. I reached out to other entrepreneurs who had been through similar challenges, and their stories of resilience were both inspiring and motivating. These stories reminded me that I wasn't alone in facing adversity, and that success often comes to those who persevere through the hardest times.

In addition to connecting with fellow entrepreneurs, I made sure to stay close to family and friends who believed in my vision. Their support was invaluable, especially on days when I doubted myself. A kind word, an uplifting message, or a simple show of faith can make all the difference in staying motivated.

**3. Celebrating Small Wins**

In the midst of big challenges, it's easy to overlook the small victories. But in my experience, it's the small wins that keep us moving forward. It might have been something as simple as perfecting a product formula, receiving positive feedback from a customer, or successfully completing a task that had been on my to-do list for weeks. Celebrating these small victories reminded me that progress was being made, even if it didn't always feel like it.

I learned to pause and acknowledge my achievements, no matter how small they seemed. These moments of recognition not only boosted my confidence but also helped me stay motivated to tackle the next challenge.

**4. Staying Connected to My "Why"**

When the going gets tough, it's essential to reconnect with your deeper purpose—the "why" behind your journey. For me, that "why" was deeply personal. It stemmed from my own health struggles, particularly my respiratory issues, and the frustration of not finding products that aligned with both my values and well-being. But my "why" didn't stop there. It also included a vision for financial stability—not just for the present but for my future. Building Caruso Valore wasn't only about creating products; it was about creating a foundation for long-term security while solving real problems for others.

Whenever I felt overwhelmed or uncertain, I would reflect on the broader impact I wanted to make. It wasn't just about developing a product line—it was about empowering others with safe, effective solutions while also creating a sustainable future for myself and my family. I wanted to ensure that Caruso Valore wasn't just a passion project but a vehicle for personal growth, financial independence, and professional legacy.

It's easy to get caught up in the day-to-day operations of running a business and lose sight of the bigger picture. But when you pause to remember why you started in the first place, it reignites your passion and motivation to keep moving forward. Whether it's the drive to solve a problem, secure your future, or leave a meaningful mark, staying connected to your "why" can provide the clarity and strength you need to navigate any challenge.

**Turning Challenges into Fuel**

One of the most powerful realizations I had during my entrepreneurial journey was that challenges, no matter how difficult, can be transformed into fuel for growth. My health challenges pushed me to think outside the box and get creative in my approach. I wasn't content to simply find a solution for myself—I wanted to create something that would serve others. And by embracing these difficulties, I was able to turn them into a source of innovation.

**The Power of Resilience**

Resilience is one of the most essential qualities an entrepreneur can cultivate. It's the ability to keep going despite setbacks, to persist even when things seem impossible. There were many times when I considered giving up—. But each time I had a setback, I reminded myself that these challenges were part of the journey. Every step forward, no matter how small, was a step closer to my goals.

I learned that resilience isn't about never facing failure; it's about facing it head-on and continuing to move forward. It's about finding the strength to keep going, even when the road ahead feels uncertain.

**Celebrating the Journey**

As entrepreneurs, we often focus so much on the destination that we forget to appreciate the journey. But every step of the journey—whether it feels like a leap forward or a stumble backward—is worth celebrating. The fact that we keep going, that we are trying, that we are putting ourselves out there and pursuing our dreams, is an accomplishment in itself.

It's important to remember that no matter where you are in your journey, you are exactly where you need to be to get to where you're going. Each experience, whether it's a triumph or a setback, is preparing you for what's next. Trust the process, embrace the challenges, and celebrate the progress you've made.

**Moving Forward with Passion**

Passion is the driving force that propels us forward, even in the face of adversity. For me, my passion for creating natural, effective products and helping others has been a constant source of motivation. It's what gets me out of bed every morning and keeps me pushing forward, even on the toughest days.

If there's one thing I hope you take away from this chapter, it's this: your journey is worth celebrating. Every challenge, every setback, and every success is a part of your story. Keep going, keep learning, and most importantly, keep believing in yourself. You are capable of achieving great things, and with each step, you're getting closer to your goals.

**Reflection Exercise: Staying Inspired**

To help you stay motivated and inspired, I encourage you to reflect on your journey so far. Consider the following prompts and write down your thoughts:

1. What inspired you to start your journey?
2. What are the biggest challenges you've faced, and how have you grown from them?
3. What is your "why"—the deeper reason behind your goals?
4. What small wins can you celebrate today?
5. How can you reconnect with your passion when things get tough?

**Action Steps to Stay Inspired and Motivated**

1. **Create a Vision Board**: Fill it with images, words, and quotes that represent your goals and dreams. Place

it somewhere visible to remind yourself of your "why."
2. **Establish a Morning Routine**: Begin each day with activities that inspire and ground you, such as journaling, meditating, or exercising.
3. **Find a Mentor**: Connect with someone who has been where you are and can provide guidance and encouragement.
4. **Set Achievable Milestones**: Break down your big goals into smaller, manageable steps. Celebrate each milestone as you reach it.
5. **Practice Gratitude**: Reflect daily on three things you're grateful for. Gratitude can shift your mindset and keep you focused on the positive aspects of your journey.

By reflecting on these questions and taking actionable steps, you can gain clarity and refocus your energy on what truly matters. Remember, every step you take is a step closer to your dreams. Trust the process, embrace the challenges, and celebrate the incredible journey you're on.

# Chapter Eleven

# Chapter Eleven

## Chapter 11: Goal Setting for Success

Success doesn't happen by accident. Whether you're just starting your entrepreneurial journey or you're a seasoned business owner looking to maintain momentum, setting clear, actionable goals is the foundation of progress. In this chapter, we will explore why goal setting is crucial, how to set goals that align with your vision, and practical strategies to ensure you stay on track. Additionally, you'll find exercises to personalize this process and discover what resonates with your unique situation and aspirations.

### Why Goal Setting is Essential

Goals provide direction. They act as a roadmap that keeps you focused and motivated, even when challenges arise. For entrepreneurs, goal setting can:

- **Clarify Priorities**: With endless tasks and opportunities, knowing where to focus your energy prevents overwhelm.

- **Measure Progress**: Goals help you track how far you've come and what's left to achieve.
- **Boost Confidence**: Reaching milestones, no matter how small, reinforces your ability to succeed.
- **Encourage Accountability**: A defined goal makes it easier to hold yourself accountable or enlist support from others.

Without clear goals, you risk wasting time on activities that don't align with your bigger vision. As an entrepreneur, this can mean the difference between growing a thriving business and stagnating.

**The Goal-Setting Process**

To create a goal-setting system that works, follow these steps:

1. **Envision Your Ideal Future**

    - Start with a vision of where you want to be in 1, 5, or 10 years. Imagine your personal and professional life. What does success look like to you? Consider your income, work-life balance,

reputation, and the impact you're making.
- Exercise: Write a "future self" letter. Describe a day in your life five years from now, focusing on what you've achieved and how you feel.

2. **Break Down the Vision into Goals**

    - Use your vision to identify specific goals that will lead you there. Separate them into short-term (6-12 months), medium-term (1-3 years), and long-term (3-10 years) categories.
    - Example:
        - Short-term: Launch a new product line.
        - Medium-term: Secure partnerships with five high-end salons.
        - Long-term: Scale your business to $1 million in annual revenue.

3. **Make Your Goals SMART**

   - Goals should be Specific, Measurable, Achievable, Relevant, and Time-bound.
   - Example:
     - Non-SMART: "Grow my business."
     - SMART: "Increase monthly revenue by 20% within the next six months by expanding my wholesale client base."

4. **Align Goals with Values**

   - Ensure your goals reflect your core values and what matters most to you. Misaligned goals can lead to burnout or dissatisfaction.
   - Exercise: List your top three personal and professional values. Check if each goal aligns with these values.

5. **Create an Action Plan**

   - Break each goal into smaller, actionable steps. Assign deadlines to each step to maintain momentum.

- Example:
  - Goal: Launch a new product line.
    - Step 1: Research market trends (Deadline: Week 1).
    - Step 2: Develop prototypes (Deadline: Week 4).
    - Step 3: Finalize packaging (Deadline: Week 6).
    - Step 4: Announce product launch (Deadline: Week 8).

6. **Track and Reflect**

    - Regularly review your goals and progress. Adjust as needed based on new opportunities or challenges.
    - Exercise: Set aside 15 minutes weekly to evaluate your progress. Use a journal or tracking app to document what worked, what didn't, and next steps.

**Examples of Goal-Setting in Action**

Here are real examples of how goal setting worked for me in my journey as an entrepreneur:

**Short-Term Goal**
When I launched Caruso Valore, one of my initial goals was to secure a handful of wholesale accounts within the first few months. While I'm still working toward this, I've made strides by identifying potential partners, crafting personalized pitches, and focusing on how my products can complement boutique shops and high-end salons. It's a goal in progress, and each connection I make gets me closer to achieving it.

**Long-Term Goal**
Scaling Caruso Valore to $1 million in annual sales remains a long-term goal. While I'm not there yet, I'm breaking it down into actionable steps, such as increasing my online store's visibility, building meaningful relationships with boutique owners and salon professionals, and creating approachable wholesale options to encourage small businesses to try my products. These milestones are a work in progress, but each step brings me closer to realizing this vision.

As you think about your own goals, be honest and true to yourself. Set objectives that align with your unique vision, your "why," and your capacity. This is not about chasing arbitrary targets or comparing yourself to others—it's about creating realistic, meaningful goals that make sense for you and your business. Remember, progress is progress, no matter how small, as long as it aligns with the bigger picture you've imagined for yourself.

**Common Challenges and How to Overcome Them**

1. **Overwhelmed by Too Many Goals**

    - Solution: Prioritize. Focus on one or two key goals at a time. Delegate or postpone less critical tasks.

2. **Fear of Failure**

    - Solution: Shift your mindset. View failures as learning opportunities. Celebrate progress, not perfection.

3. **Lack of Motivation**

    o Solution: Revisit your "why." Remind yourself why you set the goal in the first place. Surround yourself with supportive people.

4. **Procrastination**

    o Solution: Use time-blocking techniques to dedicate focused time to your goals. Break tasks into smaller, manageable pieces.

**Exercises to Align Goals with Your Situation**

1. **Vision Mapping**

    o Create a vision board using images, words, or sketches that represent your ideal future. Place it somewhere visible to keep your goals top of mind.

2. **Obstacle Identification**

    o Write down potential challenges for each goal. Then brainstorm solutions or actions to address these challenges.

3. **Reverse Engineering**

- Take a long-term goal and work backward. List the steps you would need to take to make it happen, starting from the end result and moving to the present.

4. **Accountability Partner**

    - Share one goal with a trusted friend or mentor. Set regular check-ins to discuss progress and challenges.

5. **Time Audit**

    - Track how you spend your time for a week. Identify activities that don't align with your goals and find ways to reduce or eliminate them.

**Final Thoughts on Goal Setting**

Goal setting is not a one-time activity; it's a continuous process that evolves with you and your business. By setting clear, actionable goals and committing to regular reflection, you can maintain focus and adapt to changes while staying true to your vision.

Take time to implement the exercises in this chapter and evaluate what resonates most with you. Remember, success isn't just about achieving goals—it's about growing into a person capable of achieving them.

As you finish this chapter, write down one short-term and one long-term goal you're committed to pursuing. Break them into actionable steps, and take the first step today.

# Chapter Twelve

# Chapter Twelve

### Chapter 12: Becoming or Maintaining Entrepreneurial Status

Entrepreneurship is more than a career choice; it's a mindset and a lifestyle. Whether you're striving to become an entrepreneur or you're looking to maintain and expand your status as one, this chapter will delve into the essential habits, strategies, and mindset shifts required to succeed. You will also find exercises to reflect on your unique situation and goals, helping you align your entrepreneurial journey with your long-term vision.

## The Entrepreneurial Mindset

To be an entrepreneur, you need to think like one. Entrepreneurs are problem-solvers, innovators, and risk-takers who balance optimism with realism. The mindset encompasses resilience, adaptability, and a relentless drive to create value. Below are key traits of the entrepreneurial mindset:

1. **Resilience:** The ability to bounce back from setbacks is critical. Entrepreneurship involves constant challenges, but viewing failures as learning opportunities is key to long-term success.

2. **Vision:** Entrepreneurs see opportunities where others see obstacles. They imagine the possibilities and work tirelessly to turn them into realities.

3. **Adaptability:** The business landscape is constantly changing. Entrepreneurs stay flexible, ready to pivot when needed.

4. **Focus on Value Creation:** Instead of chasing money, successful entrepreneurs focus on solving problems and adding value.

**Exercise: Develop Your Entrepreneurial Mindset**

1. Reflect on your current challenges. Write down three setbacks you've faced

and how you overcame (or could overcome) them.
2. Identify three opportunities in your industry that others might be overlooking. Brainstorm how you could capitalize on these opportunities.
3. Write a paragraph describing your vision for your business or entrepreneurial journey in the next five years.

---

## Setting Clear Goals

Entrepreneurs thrive when they have a clear roadmap. Setting specific, measurable, achievable, relevant, and time-bound (SMART) goals can help you stay focused and motivated.

**Categories of Entrepreneurial Goals**

1. **Financial Goals:** Define revenue, profit, and investment targets.
2. **Growth Goals:** Focus on market expansion, customer acquisition, or product development.
3. **Personal Development Goals:** Aim to build your skills, network, and knowledge.

4. **Impact Goals:** Consider the social or environmental impact of your business.

**Exercise: Define Your SMART Goals**

1. Write down one financial goal, one growth goal, and one personal development goal you want to achieve in the next year. Use the SMART framework to refine them.
2. Break each goal into actionable steps. For example, if your financial goal is to generate $10,000 in monthly revenue, list the actions needed to achieve that target (e.g., increasing marketing efforts, launching a new product, etc.).
3. Set deadlines for each step and track your progress weekly.

---

## Building a Support System

No entrepreneur succeeds alone. A strong support system provides advice, encouragement, and resources. Surround yourself with mentors, peers, and professionals who can guide you through challenges and celebrate your successes.

**Key Components of a Support System**

1. **Mentors:** Seek individuals with experience in your industry who can provide insights and guidance.
2. **Peers:** Join networking groups or mastermind circles to connect with like-minded entrepreneurs.
3. **Team Members:** Build a team that complements your skills and shares your vision.
4. **Friends and Family:** Maintain relationships with those who support your journey emotionally and financially.

**Exercise: Evaluate Your Support System**

1. List the people in your current support system and their roles (mentor, peer, team member, etc.).
2. Identify any gaps. For instance, do you lack a mentor in a specific area, such as marketing or finance?
3. Create an action plan to fill these gaps. Research local networking events, online communities, or professional organizations.

## Time Management and Productivity

Entrepreneurs wear many hats, making time management essential. Productivity is not about doing more; it's about focusing on what matters most.

**Strategies for Time Management**

1. **Prioritize Tasks:** Categorize tasks into urgent, important, and non-essential.
2. **Set Boundaries:** Protect your time by saying no to distractions and delegating tasks where possible.
3. **Batch Work:** Group similar tasks together to maintain focus and efficiency.
4. **Embrace Technology:** Use tools like project management software, scheduling apps, and automation to streamline your workflow.

**Exercise: Audit Your Time**

1. Track your daily activities for one week, noting how much time you spend on each task.
2. Identify activities that waste time or don't align with your goals.
3. Create a revised schedule that prioritizes high-impact tasks.

---

## Staying Motivated and Avoiding Burnout

The entrepreneurial journey is demanding, and it's easy to lose motivation or experience burnout. Staying motivated requires a balance between hard work and self-care.

### Tips for Staying Motivated

1. **Celebrate Small Wins:** Acknowledge and reward your progress, no matter how small.
2. **Reconnect with Your Why:** Remind yourself why you started your entrepreneurial journey.

3. **Invest in Self-Care:** Regular exercise, healthy eating, and sufficient sleep are non-negotiable.
4. **Seek Inspiration:** Read books, listen to podcasts, or attend events that inspire you.

**Exercise: Motivation Journal**

1. Write a journal entry about why you became (or want to become) an entrepreneur. Include your aspirations and how achieving them will impact your life and others.
2. List five ways you will celebrate your next milestone.
3. Create a self-care checklist and commit to incorporating at least one item daily.

---

## Financial Planning for Entrepreneurs

Financial management is the backbone of any successful business. Entrepreneurs must have a clear understanding of their finances to make informed decisions.

**Key Financial Practices**

1. **Budgeting:** Track your income and expenses to ensure profitability.
2. **Investing in Growth:** Allocate resources to areas with the highest return on investment.
3. **Emergency Fund:** Maintain a financial cushion for unexpected challenges.
4. **Seek Professional Advice:** Consult with accountants or financial planners to optimize your strategy.

**Exercise: Financial Health Check**

1. Review your current financial statements (or personal finances if you're starting out).
2. Identify areas where you can cut costs or increase revenue.
3. Create a 6-month financial plan, including a budget and investment strategy.

---

## Conclusion and Reflection

Becoming or maintaining entrepreneurial status requires intentionality, resilience, and a commitment to growth. By cultivating the right mindset, setting clear goals, building a support system, managing your time, staying motivated, and maintaining financial health, you can thrive as an entrepreneur.

**Final Exercise: Reflection and Commitment**

1. Reflect on what resonated most with you in this chapter. Write a paragraph about how you will apply these lessons to your journey.
2. Create a vision board or mind map that represents your entrepreneurial goals and dreams.
3. Share your vision and goals with someone in your support system, and ask for their feedback or encouragement.

Remember, entrepreneurship is a journey, not a destination. Celebrate the progress you make and stay committed to your vision.

# Chapter Thirteen

# Chapter Thirteen

**Chapter 13: Advice to My Younger Self**

If I could go back in time, I would sit my younger self down and have a heart-to-heart about what it truly means to follow a dream, what the path ahead would look like, and how to navigate the storms. The road from a job to the life of an entrepreneur isn't a straight line—it's more like a jellyfish floating in a current, trying to find its way. This chapter is for anyone feeling stuck, unsure of their purpose, or fearful of taking the leap. It's the advice I wish someone had shared with me when I was starting out. If that's you, I hope this will resonate.

---

## The Jellyfish Stage

When I think back to the early days, I often refer to them as my "jellyfish stage." At the time, I felt like I was just floating through life—drifting from one job to another without a real sense of direction. I'd go where the current took me, afraid to break away and swim on my own. If you're in this stage, know that you're not alone.

Looking back, I wish I had told myself:

- **It's okay not to have it all figured out.** Stop comparing yourself to others who seem to be miles ahead. Everyone's timeline is different.
- **Every job, even the ones you hate, is a stepping stone.** You're learning skills and building resilience, even if it doesn't feel like it right now.
- **Your worth isn't tied to your current job title.** You're more than what you do to pay the bills.

**Reflection Exercise:**

1. Write down three things you've learned from past jobs—even the ones you didn't enjoy.
2. Think about what you liked and disliked about each role. How can this guide you toward your next step?
3. If you feel adrift, describe what "anchored" success might look like for you in 5 years.

## Taking the First Leap

Starting something new—whether it's a side hustle, a business, or a major life change—is terrifying. I remember feeling paralyzed by fear, convinced that I wasn't ready. I didn't have a clear plan, and I doubted whether I was capable of building something on my own. If I could go back, I would grab myself by the shoulders and say:

- **Start before you're ready.** Perfectionism is a trap. You'll never feel 100% ready, and that's okay. Take messy action and learn as you go.
- **Trust your gut.** If an idea excites you and feels aligned with who you are, pursue it. Don't let the opinions of others dim your enthusiasm.
- **You'll figure it out.** The solutions to your problems often reveal themselves when you're in the middle of the work, not before you begin.

**Reflection Exercise:**

1. What's one idea or goal you've been sitting on because you feel unprepared? Write down the smallest first step you can take.
2. Imagine your future self has achieved this goal. What advice would they give you about starting?
3. Write down three affirmations to remind yourself that you are capable of figuring things out.

---

## The Struggles No One Tells You About

Entrepreneurship is often glamorized, but the reality is far from perfect. There were days when I wondered if I'd made the biggest mistake of my life. I faced sleepless nights, financial stress, and the nagging voice of self-doubt. Here's what I wish I'd known during those dark moments:

- **Failure is part of the process.** It's not a sign that you're on the wrong path; it's proof that you're trying.
- **You're not supposed to have all the answers.** No one does. The key is to stay curious and keep learning.

- **Asking for help is a strength, not a weakness.** Reach out to mentors, peers, or even your competitors. People are often more willing to help than you think.

**Reflection Exercise:**

1. Write down a time when you failed or felt discouraged. What did you learn from the experience?
2. List three people you can turn to for advice or support in your current journey.
3. What's one area of your business or life where you could benefit from asking for help?

---

## What I Would Say to My Younger Self

If I could sit across from my younger self, here's what I'd tell her:

- **You're stronger than you think.** You'll face challenges you can't even imagine right now, but you'll survive them all—and come out stronger.
- **Your instincts are your superpower.** You already know what's

right for you. Trust that little voice inside.
- **You don't have to do it alone.** Building a business and a life you love isn't a solo act. Surround yourself with people who believe in you.
- **Celebrate the small wins.** Don't wait until you've achieved the big goals to feel proud of yourself. Every step forward is worth celebrating.
- **Don't let fear stop you.** The fear never fully goes away, but it loses its power the moment you act in spite of it.

**Reflection Exercise:**

1. Write a letter to your younger self, sharing the advice you wish you had then.
2. Reflect on how far you've come. Write down five things you're proud of achieving.
3. List one fear or limiting belief you have right now. What action can you take today to confront it?

---

## Closing Thoughts

The journey from a job to becoming an entrepreneur is messy, unpredictable, and sometimes downright scary. But it's also one of the most rewarding things you can do. To my younger self—and to you, the reader—I want to say this: You are capable of so much more than you realize. The struggles are real, but so are the victories. Start before you're ready, keep moving forward, and never stop believing in yourself.

Entrepreneurship isn't just about building a business; it's about building yourself. And trust me, the person you become along the way is worth every single challenge.

**The Jellyfish and the Entrepreneur**

An entrepreneur's journey is much like a jellyfish gliding through the ocean. At first glance, the jellyfish may seem fragile, tossed about by the currents, with no clear direction. But in reality, it moves with purpose—pulsing forward, adapting to the ever-changing tides. Like the jellyfish, entrepreneurs must embrace uncertainty and learn to flow with the challenges they face, using each obstacle as an opportunity to propel forward.

A jellyfish doesn't resist the current—it works with it, trusting its instincts and knowing that every wave is part of the larger journey. Similarly, as an entrepreneur, there will be moments when you feel vulnerable, carried by forces beyond your control. But remember, even when the waters feel overwhelming, you have the ability to adapt, pivot, and move forward with intention.

Sometimes, that forward movement might look like stepping back from something you thought was "it." Maybe it's a business, a project, or even a career path that no longer aligns with your goals or vision. Letting go isn't failure—it's strength. It's knowing when to reevaluate, redefine, and evolve. Use the lessons you've learned to reshape your path, refine your passions, and grow into something even greater.

The jellyfish thrives by being flexible, resourceful, and resilient. In the same way, your entrepreneurial journey will require patience, courage, and trust in your vision. No matter how uncertain the waters may seem, every pulse forward—whether it's continuing, pivoting, or starting anew—brings you closer to your goals. Stay focused, embrace the flow, and trust that, like the jellyfish, you are built to navigate the tides and thrive in your own unique way.

# Chapter Fourteen

# Chapter Fourteen

**Chapter 14: Turning Dreams Into Legacy**

Building a business isn't just about the present—it's about creating something that will live on, something that reflects your values, passions, and the difference you hope to make in the world. When I think about what I've built with Caruso Valore and my salon, Studio Di Capelli, it's more than just business to me. They are reflections of the sacrifices, lessons, and love I've poured into every step of the journey. But even more than that, they're reminders of why I started in the first place.

If there's one thing I've learned, it's this: Your dreams have the power to inspire not just your own life, but the lives of those around you. And in those moments when it feels overwhelming, remember: You don't have to sprint the entire way. Sometimes, it's okay to float.

## Why I Chose to Be a Jellyfish Now and Then

For 25 years, my husband has been my biggest cheerleader. He's the one who reminded me that I didn't have to have it all together all the time—that it's okay to let the current carry me when I needed rest, reflection, or simply joy. I've embraced the idea of being a jellyfish not as a sign of giving up, but as a way to savor life.

There's a beauty in floating. In those moments, I've found clarity, creativity, and the energy to keep pushing forward. My goal has never been to just hustle endlessly. It's been to create something meaningful while still making time to enjoy life's simple pleasures—to laugh with my daughter, to spoil my grandchildren, and to provide them with experiences that light them up with joy. That's my legacy.

**Reflection Exercise:**

1. What does "floating" look like to you? Write down ways you can incorporate moments of rest and joy into your routine.
2. Think about someone who has been a cheerleader in your life. How have they

influenced you? Write them a letter of gratitude (even if you don't send it).
3. What's one experience or memory you want to create for your loved ones that will bring them joy? How can you take a step toward making it happen?

---

## The Legacy of Trying, Failing, and Succeeding

My journey hasn't been a straight line. Along the way, I've tried businesses that didn't work out—ideas that failed, ventures that lost money, and plans that didn't go as I had hoped. But each experience taught me something invaluable. They taught me resilience, creativity, and the importance of adapting when things don't go as planned.

Caruso Valore and Studio Di Capelli are the results of years of persistence, learning from failure, and never giving up on the dream of building something I could be proud of. I've learned that entrepreneurship isn't just about success; it's about the willingness to try again, to believe in yourself even when it feels impossible, and to keep moving forward.

**Reflection Exercise:**

1. Write about a time when you faced failure. What did you learn from that experience?
2. Think about an idea or dream you gave up on. Is there a way to revisit it or apply what you learned to a new endeavor?
3. List three qualities you've developed through your setbacks and how they've shaped you as a person.

---

## Your Legacy: What Will You Leave Behind?

Your journey as an entrepreneur isn't just about the money you make or the goals you achieve. It's about the mark you leave on the people around you—your family, your friends, your customers, and even those you may never meet.

Think about the legacy you want to create. Is it a business that changes lives? Is it the example you set for your children? Is it the experiences you create for your loved ones that they'll carry with them forever? Whatever it is, hold it close and let it guide you. Your legacy isn't something that happens at the end of your journey; it's something you build every single day.

**Reflection Exercise:**

1. What does the word "legacy" mean to you? Write down three ways you'd like to be remembered.
2. Think about one small action you can take today to work toward creating that legacy.
3. Imagine the impact your business or dream could have 10 years from now. Write a paragraph describing that future.

## My Final Words to You

To my readers, I want you to know this: I believe in you. Even if we've never met, I know what it's like to dream big while battling self-doubt. I know what it's like to feel overwhelmed, wondering if you're doing the right thing. And I know what it's like to fail, pick yourself back up, and try again.

If no one has told you this lately, let me be the one to say it: You are capable. You are worthy. And you have everything it takes to turn your dreams into reality. There will be moments when you doubt yourself, but I want you to hear my voice cheering you on. I'm here to remind you that you've got this.

And when it gets tough, remember to float for a little while. Give yourself permission to rest and recharge. Joy isn't just the reward for hard work; it's an essential part of the journey.

## Conclusion

Your journey as an entrepreneur will be uniquely yours, filled with its own challenges, triumphs, and moments of magic. My hope is that this book has given you tools, insights, and encouragement to take the next step with confidence and clarity.

Whatever your dreams may be, know that you are not alone. I'm rooting for you, just as my husband has rooted for me all these years. And as you build your business and your legacy, remember to cherish the moments that matter most. Because in the end, it's not just about what you create—it's about the love, joy, and inspiration you leave behind.

Now, go chase those dreams. The world is waiting for what only you can bring.

Sherry Kelly is a licensed hair stylist in two states and the owner of *Studio Di Capelli* Salon, where she has built a thriving career over the past 17 years, serving clients with passion and care. As an entrepreneur, she knows firsthand the challenges of balancing work, family, and personal goals, often juggling the demands of running a business while staying present for her loved ones.

Through her journey, she has gained valuable insights into navigating the highs and lows of entrepreneurial life, from launching new ventures to overcoming unexpected roadblocks. She is deeply committed to helping others, whether it's mentoring salon and spa owners, creating educational resources, or simply sharing lessons learned along the way in addition to caring for and nurturing her clientele in the salon.

At the heart of it all, she is driven by a desire to make a meaningful impact—helping others succeed in business while encouraging them to prioritize self-care, set boundaries, and create balance in their own lives. She believes that true success isn't just about what you achieve, but how you feel and grow along the way.

Made in the USA
Columbia, SC
15 June 2025